Table of Contents

Part 2 – Mastering the Interview

PROLOGUE
by James F. Fitzgerald

I was pleased to be asked to write this prologue by the authors, Bob and Cindy Ward. They figured that I could come up with several excellent reasons for you to read their book. And they were right in their assumption. They have written a superb book about the process of finding a job. I base my assessment on the expertise that I have acquired over the last 30 years advising people on how to find a job.

The authors have done a great job of reducing a lot of the myths and mysteries about the job search process into a book of very practical, understandable and usable recommendations. Bob has spent more than 25 years learning the realities of the interviewing process as a recruiter and executive search consultant. He has helped to place hundreds of people into all kinds of jobs. He has an excellent ability to transfer learning from one setting to another. His recommendations reflect a solid grounding in the world of interviewing. His advice rings true to me. His counsel is very practical and pragmatic.

When you have participated in as many interviews as Bob Ward has, you acquire a real sense of what works in an interview and what will kill your candidacy. It could be your appearance, how you choose to present yourself, or it could be the presentation of your "story". It could be your lack of preparation that "bites" you. It could be the way you prepared your resume. It could be your failure to understand that you are your own sales representative. It could be your lack of follow up with your prospective employer. Other things that eliminate candidates include: a failure to understand how the process works; not knowing the protocol of the interview process; not knowing how to prepare your references for those hoped-for reference calls; not using the talents of a good friend to review your resume very critically; lacking a time consciousness during the interview; failure to be succinct in your answers --- don't make a clock when you are asked the time.

Both authors have a great facility to cut through the clutter of the job search process. Both authors worked very hard on the wording of their advice.

If you want to properly prepare for your next interview, do yourself a real favor; take the time to read this excellent book. In my considered judgment, it will be time very well spent.

James F. Fitzgerald
James F. Fitzgerald & Associates, Inc.
Executive Career Transition and Coaching
Oak Brook, IL.

The very worst "F" word

Chapter 1

Introduction:
I'm your friendly headhunter
and I'm here to help...

INTERVIEW DISASTER

Interviewer:
So I see your list of accomplishments at ExecuCo includes the establishment of a Whistleblower committee...

This book is full of enlightening, life-based accounts taken straight from the experiences of its author. The following is not one of them:

It is a lazy Monday afternoon. Justin Andrews is seated on his couch accompanied only by his two-year old beagle, Sandra, and a bag of cheddar-and-sour cream potato chips. With his remote in hand, he flips through the channels on his TV, finally deciding to catch another classic episode of Judge Jezebel. Or maybe a nap is in order. After all, he has washed the breakfast dishes, sent out two resumes, and walked the dog around the perimeter of the back yard.

It is Justin's fourth week since being laid off and he has established a routine that does not include an alarm clock, a stressful commute, or a daily shower. His wife will not arrive home from work for another two hours, at which point he plans to be sitting in front of his computer looking worn out and somewhat pitiful. But meanwhile, thirty minutes of Judge Jezebel followed by forty winks seems like a plan.

His cell phone sings out "Hot Blooded" by Foreigner, startling Justin from a dream.

He picks up his phone and notes that he is being contacted by an unknown caller. Remembering that he is looking for a job, he shakes the cobwebs from his brain, mutes Judge Jezebel and answers enthusiastically, "Hello."

"Hello, I'm looking for Justin Andrews," chirps a perky female voice.

"Speaking," says Justin, suspecting that the call is his third one in a week about life insurance.

"Justin, this is Teresa Corboy from the Human Resources department at Bailey Medical Products. I wonder if I could have a few minutes of your time."

Bailey Medical Products is a direct competitor of Justin's former employer. Its office is one mile from his home. He sent the company a resume on his first day of unemployment, back when he still had hope and energy and ambition. Dream Job, whispers an inner voice. Justin experiences a sudden attack of nerves.

"Of course," he responds.

"Well, Justin, I'm happy to inform you that we have looked at the resume you sent us and are very impressed. In fact, we are so impressed with your background that we'd like to hire you as our regional sales manager."

"That's great," Justin responds. "I'm available to come for an interview..." he checks an imaginary calendar, "let's see... any morning next week."

"Oh, no need for that," laughs Teresa Corboy from Human Resources. "My boss is a good friend of your former boss. We contacted her and she had great things to say about you – you know, hard work, good time management, all that stuff. She told us that her company had

verified all your credentials when you were hired. So really, there's nothing we need to discuss. You can start next Monday if you accept the position."

"But what about salary?" Justin asks.

"Just e-mail us your salary requirements. I'm sure we can match your previous salary and even provide a small raise, perhaps as much as 10%. As a general rule, Bailey pays much more generously than your former employer. And of course you will be entitled to four weeks of vacation and full medical benefits. Beyond that, you can e-mail us any questions."

"But, shouldn't we meet..." starts Justin.

"That will not be necessary," says Teresa Corboy from Human Resources in a firm voice. "Your office is waiting. We'll see you Monday unless we hear otherwise."

The previous scenario is fictional, make-believe, imaginary, phony. It will never, never, NEVER, NEVER happen. It will never happen because of Interview Truth Number One.

Interview Truth Number One:
Behind every fantastic job is a successful job interview

Unless you are one of a loyal group of my friends and supporters numbering in the single digits, you are probably reading these words because you are looking for a job or at least thinking about it. You may be unemployed or unhappily employed. You may be hoping to climb up the corporate ladder – or trying to make it to the bottom rung. Whatever the case, you will not be able to secure the job you want without first securing and surviving a job interview. Few people love job interviewing. But the fact is, getting hired into even the lowest level position will require a face-to-face meeting and the ability to answer a few questions.

Since you have picked up this interview book, it is reasonable to assume that you have some doubts about your interviewing skills.

Doubt not. With a little time and preparation, you can become an interview master. I'm your friendly headhunter and I'm here to help.

Having been an executive search professional (headhunter) for over 25 years, I know the interviewing process only too well. My career has allowed me to participate in the employment searches of hundreds of individuals. I have read reams of resumes, recruited men and women from across the nation, and participated personally in countless interviews. I have guided candidates through the interview process. And I have been entrusted to convey the happy or too-often disappointing results that await each candidate at the conclusion of an interview.

It is an unfortunate fact that, for every job opportunity, many are called (witness my telephone bill) and only one is chosen. In a tight job market, every rejection represents a precious opportunity lost. A rejection due to poor interviewing skills is even more regrettable because it might have been avoidable through coaching and preparation.

I believe that I have helped many candidates succeed at their interviews. I want to help you succeed at your interviews too. Throughout this book, I will attempt to offer you the same guidance I have been giving my candidates for over 25 years. Additionally I will use true-life interview scenarios to illustrate my advice, based upon the idea that it is always easier to recognize a mistake when it is someone else's.

Of course, your experience to date may be so great that you need not concern yourself with trivialities such as interviewing skills. Wrong.

Interview Truth Number Two:
Outstanding career ≠ outstanding interview

Year after year, I have been forced to watch as even accomplished professionals struggle with poor interviewing abilities.

I try to remind my candidates that an interview is just two people having a conversation. Nevertheless, even high achievers and Mensa qualifiers can turn into muddled, befuddled messes when faced with the interrogation techniques of…THE INTERVIEWER. It never ceases to surprise me when an individual who can direct a company's finances, produce written reports that would put this book's authors to shame, or manage a large staff of professionals, stumbles awkwardly to answer an interviewer's questions.

Familiarity with the interview process can increase a candidate's comfort level and confidence, thereby improving his or her interview performance. The following chapters address such topics as interview preparation, appropriate attire, commonly asked interview questions, challenging interview situations, follow-up, offer negotiations and more. If you are an interviewing novice or haven't had a job interview in fourteen years, this information can open your eyes as to what you should expect. If you are an experienced interviewer, the chapters can commit you to the right track or offer an opportunity for behavior modification if you have developed some bad habits.

Of course, you cannot expect miracles from the pages of a book. No sentence in Chapter 7 or Chapter 11 will help a bad accountant get hired to a CFO position. Still, what I have learned over the course of many interviews might just help you survive one or two. In the 21st century, people don't remain in the same job forever. Like it or not - job interviews are facts of life…..

Interview Truth Number Three:
Death, taxes and job interviews are 3 inescapable facts of life

Unless you are a wealthy heir or heiress, a member of the monarchy, or the son, daughter, niece, nephew, parent, cousin, lover, or ghost payroller of a powerful politician, at some point in your life, you are going to have to submit to a job interview.

I tell my candidates that the interview process is like filing a tax return. It is painful, time-consuming, and unavoidable.

But here's the difference. A tax return is filed every year. On April 14, you just might remember enough from the previous year to enable you to get through the ugly process without a major crisis or a heated argument with your spouse. But imagine if tax returns were filed only every five years - yes, I'm smiling with you. Each tax filing would find you starting from scratch, and perhaps scratching your head, with little or no recollection of your last filing. *("Let's see – what was that educational deduction I took back in 2005?")* Since few people execute a job search on an annual basis, most job seekers start from scratch each time they begin the interviewing process. (*"Let's see – how do I handle conflict resolution?"*)

In interviewing and taxes, practice makes perfect. Unfortunately, most individuals get their only interviewing practice on a prospective employer when the stakes are high. Since practice may not be practical, my advice is to substitute preparation for practice. This book will help you prepare for your interview. In it, I will attempt to guide you from first impression to final offer – assuming, of course, that your first impression makes the cut.....

Interview Truth Number Four:
A failed first impression is a last impression

*M**any years ago,** before establishing my own practice, I was a partner in a large, national recruiting firm that required me to log in a specific number of new, business-related acquaintances each week. The idea, which had merit, was that some percentage of these acquaintances would eventually become valuable contacts as candidates or clients.*

As a result of several recruiting calls, I invited a promising, local candidate to meet with me regarding opportunities in the finance field. We arranged to meet in my office the following day. He arrived right on time.

When I greeted this young man, I noted that his attire and personal grooming were somewhat sloppy. His collar was soiled. His hair cried out for a shampoo and a touch-up with a comb. His handshake was feeble, leaving me wondering if he lacked muscle or bones in his hand. The candidate did not meet my eyes, instead looking off to the side as he introduced himself.

At this point, before sixty seconds had passed or twenty words had been spoken, this man who was placing himself in the job market had surrendered his one and only chance to make a positive first impression on someone who might hold a key to that job. That would be me.

However, having gleaned from his resume that the candidate had great potential, I decided to see if he could be a Phoenix and rise from the ashes. I proceeded to engage him in conversation about his experience to date. Unfortunately, his continuing lackluster communication skills and low energy level only served to confirm my initial impressions

My frustration rising, I recognized that this well qualified young professional was going to be met with rejection because of messy hair, a limp handshake, and a droning speaking style. I could not recommend this man to any of my clients. From my perspective, efficient time management demanded that I cut my losses and end the conversation as quickly as possible.

Instead, I broke an unwritten rule in the business. I cut short the question-and-answer session and began to deliver a frustration-induced lecture to this unsuspecting candidate. Without solicitation, I began to tell this man what he was doing wrong and what he should be doing instead. I covered interview behavior from the initial greeting to likely questions to the final handshake, allowing for little or no response from the candidate. I made it my personal project to turn around this candidate's interview performance. At the end of my tirade, the beaten-down man rather sheepishly got up from the table, thanked me (!?) for my time and left.

Within minutes, I began to second-guess myself. My best career interests are served by making friends with as many people as possible.

My best interests definitely are not served by creating enemies. Although meant to be constructive, my suggestions had sounded a lot like insults, even to my ear. An onslaught of criticism to this candidate, even well-intentioned criticism, might not have won me a friend or a future referral.

I managed to forgive myself (being an expert at self-forgiveness) and moved on. Several weeks later, I received a surprising phone call. My "project" candidate was on the line, following up to tell me he had just accepted a very nice job. I cringed, waiting for the unavoidable "Pound sand!" or worse. Instead, the young man sincerely thanked me. He had implemented my suggestions regarding his interview style and credited his new presentation skills with helping him to win his new position.

I gave myself a pat on the back and spent several minutes basking in the glow of having helped someone, though admittedly my motivation may not have been perfect. Then, it was back to work, as I don't earn a fee for basking in the glow.

As is demonstrated by my bad-hair candidate, skills and experience alone do not get you a job. You may be the most qualified candidate west or east of the Mississippi, yet lose an opportunity because of your bad taste in ties or a weak handshake or a bit of undetected spaghetti sauce on your cuff.

Your first impression MUST be impressive in order for you to proceed to a new job. Throughout this book, I hope to help you avoid small mistakes in interview appearance and demeanor. These seemingly minor errors can cost you the opportunity of moving beyond the first impression.

And after that, your interviewing excellence must continue if you are to beat out the stiff competition for every position.....

Interview Truth Number Five
A superior interview can trump a superior background

Surprisingly, I have witnessed many cases in which the expected outcome of a series of interviews differs from the actual outcome. The unexpected conclusion is usually the result of a good candidate communicating poorly during an interview or a perceived lesser candidate performing brilliantly.

*M**any years back, I was retained to fill a VP of Finance position for a subsidiary of a foreign pharmaceutical company. The management of the company requested that I screen my entire pool of candidates and present them with the top five. I spent weeks doing research, making phone calls, examining resumes, meeting potential candidates, eliminating some, and ultimately selecting the five best people to present to my client.*

In the process of scheduling the initial interviews with the client, one of my five candidates pulled herself from contention. At this point in the process, time was of the essence. I inserted my number six candidate into the schedule.

Candidate Six was Jack Dooley. Jack was well qualified for the position, but did not have the exact background specified by the company in its position requirements. Still, I felt he would be capable of handling the job, so, in a rushed situation, I did not hesitate to substitute him for the other candidate.

At the interview, Jack Dooley performed like a rock star, explaining his previous responsibilities and how they would transfer to the current role. Any doubts the employer had about deficiencies in Jack's background were swiftly eliminated. In the end, his near-perfect presentation convinced the interviewers, and he was awarded the position over four seemingly more qualified candidates.

An exceptional interview will not always propel you to the top of the heap in a group of more qualified candidates. But a horrible interview will almost always land you at the bottom, even if you are the most qualified candidate.

---SUMMARY---

In days of job scarcity and high unemployment, it is more important than ever to know how to find and secure the position you are seeking. Whether you are a recent graduate seeking a first job, a seasoned professional hoping to advance your career through a job change, or the unfortunate individual who has been impacted by a job loss, in this environment, you will face significant competition for every available position.

> *But, as challenging as the economic climate may be, it is never - repeat never - impossible to find a job.*

People are promoted. People relocate. People retire. People are fired. People die. People go to jail. Companies disband. Companies re-organize. New companies are formed. All of these events occur whether the economy is soaring or slinking its way through a recession. In many of these cases, a position is created or left vacant. This position may be the one you seek.

Chapters 2 through 5 of this book will focus on how to seek and obtain a job interview. In these chapters, I will pass on some ideas about targeting the job you want and creating a strategy to get invited to interview for that job. Topics include: self-evaluation, preparation of a resume, use of technology, personal networking, use of recruiters, and conducting research.

But, as the book's title suggests, the primary reason I am writing this book, is to help you prepare for the interview you must eventually have in order to land in the position you want. Chapters 6 through 16 of the book will deal with the actual interview process from first contact to tough questions to negotiating your offer.

Many people might consider a third degree burn preferable to a job interview. But the interviewing process need not be an occasion of torture. In fact it can actually be fun, or so I tell my candidates (in the most sincere and persuasive tone imaginable). Like it or not, a job search is one of the few chances in life to redirect your future and change your life in a meaningful way. Being prepared for your job interview is one way of taking charge of that process and achieving the future you deserve.

INTERVIEW MASTER

Interviewer:
To tell you the truth, Ellen, I was a little concerned about your lack of experience within an insurance company such as this one. But you have persuaded me that your consulting experience in the insurance industry transfers very nicely to our environment.

Hello, I'm your friendly headhunter. Let's begin with a visualization exercise. First, close your eyes and pretend you want to be here.

Chapter 2

Self-Evaluation:
Exposing Your Hard Wiring

INTERVIEW DISASTER

Interviewer:
I see that you have a degree in engineering, a master's degree in political science, a full-time MBA with an accounting emphasis...and now you are here interviewing for our marketing position. Describe how your education has helped you to establish a direction for your career.

Candidate:
I have established that I love going to school – not so much the whole 9 to 5 routine. That gets old really fast. As soon as I have saved enough money, I'm off to law school.

At some point in your career, you may experience a FLASH! moment that leaves you wondering if the path you are on will ultimately lead to your success and happiness.

The FLASH! moment may be rooted in something external: a job termination; a confrontation with a boss; recognition of yourself in a Dilbert cartoon; a conversation with a friend; or a call from a headhunter.

Or the FLASH! moment may simply occur without warning or explanation. One day you are more or less happily performing your job duties. The next, you are mad as hell and not going to take it anymore. Call it a personal awakening; call it your boss's worst nightmare.

When the motivation for change is sudden and perhaps outside of your control, as in a job loss, the natural inclination is to race into action without delay. You feel unsettled and you don't like that unsettled feeling. *What do you want? A NEW JOB! When do you want it? NOW!*

You may find yourself rapidly scanning dozens of online job sites and reading hundreds of position descriptions; writing and re-writing your resume; studying article after article and book after book about the job search process; sending out e-mails to everyone you have known since the fifth grade.

Take this advice from one who occasionally spins his wheels. Stop spinning your wheels.

Before you look at the job boards; before you go to the office supply store; before you buy the latest "how to" resume book; before you start networking; just **STOP**.

> *You do not get an infinite number of chances in life to change course. A job or career change, whether voluntary or involuntary, is one of those infrequent chances. As you embark on this process, try to relax enough to allow yourself the luxury of a little self-examination.*

Before you set out on the next step into your future, decide what you want that future to be. Make an effort to gain some understanding of what you like doing and what you are suited to do. How are you wired as a person? Who are you? (If the answer is, someone who does not like working, keep in mind that the supply of wealthy heirs and heiresses to marry is limited.)

Most of us do not know who we are when we start our careers. We have graduated from high school or college or graduate school. During our schooling, in addition to some subject matter, we have learned a great deal – about alcohol and members of the opposite sex - and at least a little about life in general. At some point we have chosen a major, perhaps based on the objective of growing rich, perhaps based on advice from a parent or family member, perhaps based on a passionate interest in the ancient Mayan culture. Then, suddenly, our parents have relinquished financial responsibility for us and *WE NEED MONEY*. In many cases, we take the first job we are offered that *PAYS MONEY*.

This first job that we accept because of the need to nourish ourselves and dress in warm clothes often sets the direction for the rest our adult lives. That direction might be into sales, manufacturing, finance, law, medicine, marketing, pursuing a trade. That direction might actually be the wrong direction.

I have had many conversations with physicians, lawyers and other professionals, individuals whom you might expect to be delighted with their lives and their success, who believe that they somehow ended up on the wrong path to personal fulfillment. They may have acquired wealth, prestige, even a corner office overlooking Lake Michigan, but they left their passion and drive somewhere behind them.

So when you have the opportunity to chart a new direction or to veer even slightly from the path you have chosen, take the time to put your blinkers on and do it right. Remember that you have control of your future. If you do not like what you are doing now, you can change. If you love what you do now, figure out how to take the next step forward in the same area. A little bit of time spent now can literally change your future.

Take me, for example...

My own situation is a perfect example of changing direction midway through a career and making it work.

T **hirty-some years ago,** *I left the University of Notre Dame with my diploma clutched tightly in my freckled fist and my soon-to-make-me-wealthy accounting degree in my pocket. I accepted a position with a Big 8 (now Big 4) accounting firm, where I remained for several years, then took a position as controller for a local retailer. For a total of ten years, I was involved in various accounting-related roles.*

As it turned out, trying to make myself into an accountant was like trying to turn a hummingbird into a house pet. It just wasn't going to happen.

While trying to wean myself from a straight accounting role into a more wide-ranging managerial role, I became involved in an entrepreneurial venture. Because this venture was very small, I was forced into doing some sales and business development. Much to my surprise, although it should have been obvious to anyone who knew me for over twelve minutes, I discovered that I am a salesman.

Although that particular entrepreneurial venture was not wildly successful, the realization that I could sell and enjoyed selling has led to an enduring career in the executive search business. By choosing executive search, and initially concentrating my practice in finance-related positions, I did not have to completely retool my knowledge base. I was able to take everything that I had learned over the course of ten years in accounting and utilize that knowledge to create a new niche for myself.

My soul search was forced upon me by the requirements of an entrepreneurial enterprise. You can elect to do this search at your convenience. I guarantee you that your enjoyment of your life's work will be greatly enhanced if you can match your personal hard wiring to what you do for a living. So how do you begin the process of discernment? I have a two-part exercise that will help.

Imagine a beautiful evening in your lush backyard just as the summer blooms have made their first appearance of the year. You are sitting in your favorite chair enjoying a glass of very subtle red (not white) wine. For one evening you are free to explore the depths of your mind for the blueprints of your personal hard wiring. Don't screw up a great evening or great wine. Enjoy yourself! The next day, begin this two-part exercise.

---STEP 1: PERSONAL EXAMINATION---

Sit in a room with no distractions; no television, no IPod, no talk radio, and no romantic interest. (Warning - you may experience withdrawal symptoms at this point. Do not - repeat - do not grab any remotes.)

Begin to evaluate your strengths and weaknesses. Think about the parts of your current or previous job that are rewarding and those that cause you anxiety or stress. Examine your goals and your drivers. Some examples of questions you might ask yourself are these:

A Not-All-Inclusive Personal Examination Survey

⇒ AM I A GOOD WRITER, GOOD WITH NUMBERS?
These traits may be, but are not necessarily mutually exclusive. If you can't figure out the amount you would pay on a pair of shoes after a 25% discount, you will never be a CFO. If you cannot sign a birthday card without a grammatical error, you may want to avoid producing advertising or marketing brochures.

⇒ AM I A GOOD SPEAKER?
Sometimes, the ability to speak articulately and persuasively, i.e. B.S., can mask small deficiencies in other areas.

⇒ WHAT DO PEOPLE SAY ABOUT ME?
Do people compliment you on your mechanical abilities, your artistic talent,

your creativity, your outgoing nature, your self-awareness, and/or your powers of persuasion? What are the things people have said about you throughout your life

⇒ AM I EXCITED BY SOLVING COMPLEX PROBLEMS?
My wife can sit at the computer for hours focused on research and problem solving. I need to receive or initiate a phone call at least twice an hour.

⇒ AM I GOOD AT MANAGING PEOPLE?
It doesn't take a neurosurgeon to have a good common-sense feel for what makes people tick. If you have intuition, perceptiveness, and empathy, you might be suited for a people management role.

⇒ DO I LIKE WORKING ON THE ROAD; OR DO I LIKE A DESK AND A DAILY ROUTINE?
Most of us who have been cubicle-confined for any extended length of time picture ourselves on the road, taking numerous coffee breaks, reporting to no one, a veritable drifter being paid big bucks. Now think about snow storms, airport lines, traffic jams, flight delays, hours of solitude, scheduling and re-scheduling appointments. That cubicle with the family picture on the desk may start looking nice and cozy.

⇒ DO I APPEAR CONFIDENT TO OTHERS?
Perceived confidence is a significant attribute in many areas, including sales and management.

⇒ AM I SHY OR TIMID?
There is nothing wrong with being quiet. Do not limit yourself to underling roles because of your unassuming nature. But you may want to choose an area in which your talents and aptitudes are so apparent that they speak for themselves. A reserved, but intelligent or creative or hard-working employee can be an employer's greatest resource.

⇒ AM I A RISK TAKER OR A RISK AVOIDER?
You may be a persuasive communicator, but if you are risk averse, you probably will not survive the stress of a commissioned sales position or an entrepreneurial venture. No amount of antacid will calm the stomach of a risk avoider when the paycheck is two months late.

⇒ AM I A VISIONARY OR AN EXECUTOR?
   This is an especially important question as a career progresses into its middle
   and later years. A visionary is someone who sees assets, resources, and
   scenarios that others don't. Those visions lead to plans of action that benefit
   stake holders and possibly, mankind. Think Steve Jobs of Apple fame. An
   executor, on the other hand, is outstanding at executing the visions of
   someone else. I am an executor. My neighbor is a visionary real estate
   developer. I look at a field of grass and wonder who is going to mow it. He
   looks at the same field and sees stores, housing and a church. Without the
   ideas of visionaries, we executors have nothing to execute.

⇒ AM I A LEADER OR A FOLLOWER?
   There are very capable individuals who are neither qualified for nor
   comfortable with leadership roles.

⇒ DO I PREFER A SMALL COMPANY OR A LARGE COMPANY?
   While some prefer the intimacy of a small company environment, others
   enjoy the magnitude of a giant worldwide enterprise. It may be difficult to
   answer this question unless you have experienced both.

⇒ AM I MOTIVATED BY WEALTH?
   Is wealth your primary motivator? I hesitate to mention this because the
   money you make is absolutely no guarantee of personal fulfillment or
   happiness on the job. But the lack of wealth may be unacceptable to you. Be
   honest with yourself. You may love the image of yourself as a barista or
   freelance writer, but not so much the image of an out-of-fashion wardrobe
   and a dinky apartment.

These suggestions for self examination are only the beginning.
You should analyze your childhood, your personality, your likes and
dislikes, your previous jobs, your successes and failures.

Write your thoughts down in an organized fashion and let the list
sit for a day or two. Then revisit and revise your list. Try to be honest with
yourself. Create a realistic picture of who you are, not some impressionist
image of who you would like to be.

After you have completed Step 1 in our two-part exercise, you may believe that you have a complete understanding of who you are and what you should do with your life. You may be right or you may be wrong. You will not know until you have completed Step 2.

Warning – Step 1 was the fun part (or as fun as it gets). Step 2 is the hard part.

---STEP 2: THE HARD PART---

Step 2 is the dreaded.....asking for advice.

Sometimes, a close friend, spouse, co-worker, former employer or family member can observe things about us that we ourselves cannot see.

Choose someone you trust and let him or her know about your self-evaluation. Ask what your friend views as your strengths. Ask what your friend could envision you doing as a career. Discuss your tentative plans for the future. If your friend's ideas differ widely from yours, ask yourself why. Be open to change. Seek a second opinion. If two or more people share the same opinion of you, assume there is some justification for that opinion.

If you are not comfortable sharing your private self-evaluation with friends or family members, fee-based, professional career coaches are capable of providing great insight. If you are being laid off, career coach services may be available through your current company's benefit programs. A professional career coach can organize and clarify your thought process and provide a decision-making mechanism that will serve your needs. A good coach will challenge your thinking and lead you to make honest evaluations.

Finally, psychological/career aptitude testing is available from a number of sources. While these tests are not designed to give foolproof advice regarding your future, they can help to determine your strengths, tendencies, drivers, likes and dislikes.

To find a career coach or a source for aptitude testing, simply perform an internet search, using the words "career coach" or "career testing" or "career consulting" plus the desired city or town. If possible, it is always better to get a personal recommendation.

A ***close friend of mine*** *had been a very successful sales professional for years. His substantial annual income reflected his rare ability to sell complex services to high level executives. After several years of successful selling, he decided to make a career change. He partnered with a colleague, purchasing a company related to their field of expertise.*

My friend ultimately became responsible for marketing and general management for the firm. He was no longer out in the field, meeting with client personnel. While he was able to meet the requirements of his position, he had diverged from the area in which he excelled. In my mind, he suffered a huge personal opportunity cost by separating himself from the direct sales function. In a weak economy, both he and his company were struggling.

In a frank conversation regarding his career, he asked my opinion. My advice was blunt. Sell the company and get back into sales where you belong.

Eventually, my friend did sell the company. He has now returned to a front line sales function where he is back on track.

Be proactive in reaching out to a trusted friend for advice. Keep in mind that not all friends will have the nerve to hit you between the eyes with the brute force of bold truth. In return for their frankness, you must not hold their honest impressions against them. With an open mind and a good friend, you may learn a great deal about yourself.

---SUMMARY---

I cannot over-emphasize the need for self-analysis before you start any job search. Whether you have been laid off or are simply unhappy with your existing situation, a contributing factor may be a lack of "fit" with your current career path.

Take some time to evaluate your strengths and weaknesses. Approach friends and family, seeking their input.

At the end of the day, you alone are responsible for making the choices that determine your future.

If you have decided to stay the course, then approach the future on the path you have already begun. If you want to change course and can do so responsibly, go forth and change. Armed with the confidence of your self-evaluation and the affirmation of others, you can begin the steps toward accomplishing your goal of obtaining a new job.

INTERVIEW MASTER

Candidate:
I believe that my background as an obstetric nurse will serve me well in marketing MedStuff's new line of infant care supplies to hospitals.

Chapter 3

The Resume:
Creating a Document
that Tells and Sells

INTERVIEW DISASTER

Interviewer:
I just noticed that there is a gap of five years on your resume.

Candidate:
I decided not to list my work in the laundry while I was a five-to-seven year guest of the state.

Before you can successfully present yourself at your job interview, you must first be invited to that interview. In order to be invited for an interview, you must first successfully present your background on your resume, which must then find its way into the hands of a potential employer. The truth is, without a clear, well-organized resume, you will not even get the chance to be considered for an open position.

So, although resume design is not the primary focus of this book, it is a topic that I do want to address briefly. In this chapter, I will give you some advice on how to compile and format your background into a readable document that can get you invited to a job interview.

---WHO SHOULD HAVE A RESUME?---

If you are: unemployed; unhappy at your job; bored with your job; not busy at your job; tired of your commute; ambitious; unfulfilled; open to change; in an inappropriate relationship with your co-worker; in a constant war with your boss; in a failing company; worried about losing your job; hoping to change careers; hoping to expand your knowledge base; optimistic or pessimistic about your future;

Get thee a resume! Quickly!

In a perfect world, every working adult would be prepared with an up-to-date resume at all times, just in case that once-in-a-lifetime opportunity (or friendly headhunter) comes knocking and won't be kept waiting.

But in an imperfect world, a significant number of people I have contacted over the years have required several days to come up with even bare-bones resumes. Here's a thought to ponder: In the time that I wait for one terrific candidate to prepare a resume, another equally qualified candidate may be chosen for the position and a great opportunity lost forever.

I know, I know. There are many reasons to put off writing a resume.

Perhaps you have a lengthy career – who can remember the important things you achieved way back in that first position 20-some years ago? (Who can remember what you wore to work yesterday?)

Or maybe you have a very short or entry level career – you wonder how you will manage to fill up even a single page.

Perhaps your background includes a large number of job changes – how are you going to explain those three consecutive 8-month stints?

Allow me to help you get started with some words of comfort: There is no such thing as the perfect background or the perfectly hopeless background.

> *Each individual has a unique background. No individual has a flawless background. In fact, there are almost as many different career tracks as there are dollars in the federal deficit. Your resume, once you force yourself to write it, will be neither the best nor the worst that has ever been written.*

If anxiety about some element of your background is keeping you from putting together a resume, get over it. Chances are, once you take the time to list the good things you have done, you will see that your achievements outweigh your shortcomings and you will begin to feel good about yourself.

---WHAT FORMAT IS BEST?---

There are many ways to format a resume.

I know this because I receive at least twenty resumes daily via e-mail from various recruitment websites or directly from individuals. Some resumes are in 12-point type, some in 9-point. Some use Times New Roman font, some use Arial. Some begin with a person's educational credentials, others begin with his or her most recent position, and still others start with a career or personal summary. Some are strictly functional, providing no company names.

There is no single resume format that works. If you ask ten "experts" what the best format is, you will get eleven responses (especially if there is an economist in the pack). I will examine any resume that comes my way as long as it is well-organized and easily readable. I will follow up with any person whose qualifications match up with those I am seeking, as long as I can discern that fact. However, I may immediately discard a resume in which the information most important to me is not included or is difficult to find.

Following are a few sample resumes and my observations regarding the content and format of each. These examples can help you start the resume building process.

---SAMPLE RESUME FORMATS---

My retained executive search firm, Ward & Associates, is hired by a company to recruit a number of people to be considered for a specific position. Because we receive resumes in a variety of styles and formats, we generally re-work all resumes into a consistent format before sending them to our clients. This makes it easy for our clients to compare apples with apples, education to education, credentials to credentials, without too much effort.

Following is a resume configured in the format we present to our clients.

Sample Resume #1 (Good):
Ward & Associates Format
(See next page)

RESUME OF:
CAROLYN JOHNSON
(Insert contact information here)

EDUCATION:

2002   **University of Chicago Graduate School of Business,** Chicago, Illinois
Masters of Business Administration -- Accounting

1994   **Indiana University Kelley School of Business,** Bloomington, Indiana
Bachelor of Science -- Accounting

CERTIFICATIONS:

- Certified Public Accountant (CPA) – Passed all four parts on first attempt
- Certified in Production and Inventory Management (CPIM) – Passed all six parts on first attempt

EXPERIENCE:

Jan 2005   **WONDERFUL WIDGETS, INC,** Wheaton, Illinois
To Present

Controller

Manage the accounting and information technology departments for an $80 million division of a $400 million publicly traded manufacturing corporation. Participate as a key member of the corporate senior management team.

Responsibilities include:
- Develop corporate strategy in conjunction with other members of corporate senior management team.
- Oversee internal and external audit processes on a quarterly and annual basis (including Sarbanes Oxley).
- Assist in preparing the annual 10K and quarterly 10-Q.
- Create and maintain internal controls throughout the company.
- Direct integration of recent acquisitions and product line transfers.
- Prepare annual budgets and conduct financial analyses for senior management.
- Conduct internal audits at various international locations and support president of the international division.
- Assist with managing the overall operations of the division (production, supply chain management, HR).

Accomplishments:
- Developed a pricing model that allowed salesmen to structure large transactions with maximum flexibility for the customer while maintaining acceptable profit margins.
- Led the team that upgraded the IT system from Antique Systems to Most Impressive.

Jan 2001   **INGOODCOMPANY, INC.,** Indianapolis, Indiana
To Dec 2004

Assistant Controller

Managed the accounting group for a $200 million privately held manufacturing company. Responsibilities included managing monthly accounting cycle and presenting analysis of financial statements to CFO and President.

Accomplishments:
- Created a comprehensive set of performance metrics to manage and track progress against corporate strategy.
- Provided president with blueprint for corporate restructuring, resulting in over $1 million cost reduction.
- Led the design and implementation of company-wide activity-based costing system, yielding better insight to primary cost drivers and profit margin by product.

March 1997   **BIG 4 PUBLIC ACCOUNTING,** Chicago, Illinois
To Jan 2001

etc.etc.etc. (edited for space reasons)

Notes on Sample Resume #1

Carolyn Johnson has an enviable resume for a financial professional. Her background demonstrates a clear track record of progress, and includes professional certifications, a stint in a Big 4 public accounting firm and an MBA from an elite school. Here are some reasons this resume works:

- This resume begins with the candidate's impressive education credentials and certification, and then lists her experience in reverse chronological fashion from her most recent position to the beginning of her career. An individual with less noteworthy education credentials and remarkable career achievements might begin with the career chronology.
- The dates of employment are clearly visible down the left margin, Company names are highlighted in bold type and capitals. An employer can easily scan the candidate's track record of employment at a glance and determine if it warrants further examination.
- The candidate provides a brief description of each of her employers, including company size and industry. This is helpful to an employer in determining the nature and substance of the candidate's responsibilities.
- Generally speaking, a combination of paragraph and bullet formatting makes a resume more readable than exclusive use of one or the other. Long paragraphs are cumbersome. Bullets are useful to emphasize achievements, but too many bullets may minimize the impact of each "real" achievement. No one has 21 important accomplishments in one job. Ideally, there should be a balance between the use of paragraphs and bullet points.
- The candidate's most recent positions are described in the most detail. Descriptions of responsibilities should be shorter as dates get less recent, unless those responsibilities are specifically relevant to the position being sought.

Sample Resume #2 (Good): A Sales Resume

Johann Strauss
(contact information here)

PROFILE

- Strong background in all phases of consultative selling, from strategic planning, lead generation and territory development to closing, client service and account penetration.
- Special expertise in diagnostic medical imaging and new technology introductions. Expertise in hospital, specialty physician practices, clinical departments, IT networks and best practice facilities. Successfully manage the sales cycle from initial contact through implementation.
- Closed record 10 new healthcare contracts as Healthcare Sales Manager (2008). First in company to place equipment at University of Wisconsin and University of Minnesota as Imaging Solutions Specialist. (2006). Created pipeline of $1,900,000+ as Senior Sales Executive (2002-2005).

EXPERIENCE

Healthcare Sales Manager
HEALTH-AME, INC. Minneapolis, MN   Feb. 2007-Present

Managed sales of web-based HIS-integrated ASP application to hospital and healthcare market.
- Led Healthcare Division Sales in 2008. Opened record number of 10 new healthcare user contracts during Q3 '08, specializing in large radiology/imaging groups nationally.
- Successfully introduced front-end patient financial risk assessment, demographics and eligibility solutions to integration partners and top 100 Healthcare IDNs.
- Implemented multi-level sales approach that targeted high-level decision makers, including CFO, Revenue Cycle Management, and IT Departments.
- Worked with vendor partners including WebMD, Eclipsys, Epic Systems, PerSe Technologies, and Cerner, on services offering and integrations to large IDN organizations. Initiated and presented to major stakeholders at multiple levels and departments to gain project approvals, and capital budgeting. Provide compelling ROI and process improvements to Healthcare Revenue Cycle performance

Imaging Solutions Specialist
INSTA-SOUND, INC.,   Los Angeles, CA   2006

Provided sales and service of GE Ultrasound Equipment and Telemedicine systems.
- Developed eight-state region in upper-Midwest territory. Maximized sales and productivity with territory management that effectively qualified accounts.
- Demonstrated digital image management capabilities, case selection, and telemedicine to specialists. Mastered complex Veterinary Imaging technology to qualify as Specialist.
- Opened and developed reference accounts, including University of Wisconsin and University of Minnesota selling initial systems for company.

Senior Sales Executive
BURKHARDT COMPANY   Minneapolis, MN   2002-2005

Provided sales and marketing of new, FDA-approved **3-D medical modeling** technology.
- Developed market and national/global territory with strategic planning, direct contact, tradeshows, and reference sites. Opened accounts and created pipeline for 9-12 month sales cycle.
- Developed relationships with national leaders in diagnostic radiology, neurology, plastic surgery, orthopedics, and surgical devices.
- Prospected for and developed clinical partners/customers at such leading medical institutions as Mayo Clinic, Bethesda National Naval Medical Center, UCLA, Stanford and University of Minnesota.

Continued, Page 2

Sales Resume, continued:

Johann Strauss Resume
Page 2

<u>Manufacturers' Representative</u>
ULTRINSIC SOLUTIONS   Minneapolis, MN   1995-2002

Developed territory, sold and serviced accounts for Toshiba ultrasound equipment.
- Built sales in six-state territory from scratch to $800,000. Opened and managed 30+ accounts.
- Clinical areas included radiology, OB/GYN, surgical, urology and ER.
- Successfully established key reference sites and educational partnership with University of Minnesota, which led to multiple system sales.
- Sold most systems to single reference site (eight to Mayo Clinic).
- Provided training programs to maximize equipment utilization and client satisfaction.

Prior experience as <u>Sales Representative</u> for HarmonJames Foundry Co., Racine, WI (promoted from among 30 reps to manage sales in most-vital territory; grew revenue by 20%, to nearly $4 million, despite recession). Also served as <u>Sales and Marketing Representative</u> for Kindred Oil, Inc., Lexington, KY (conducted marketing research for $750,000 expansion and exceeded all sales goals).

EDUCATION/TRAINING

- BS: Business Administration (Finance/Marketing), Univ. of Missouri, Columbia, MO (1987).

PROFESSIONAL DEVELOPMENT

- Completed medical training in numerous modalities, including ultrasound, X-ray for technologists, CT, R&F and teleradiology/PACS.
- Computer skills include Windows, ACT, GoldMine, Salesforce.com, Microsoft Office (especially PowerPoint and Word) and Internet research, including Dornfest and Billians.

Notes on Sample Resume #2

Johann Strauss is a successful sales professional with over 20 years of experience. This resume, while formatted differently from Sample Resume #1, is equally clear and attractive, thus demonstrating that there is no one perfect format. Here are some observations on this resume:

- Note that Johann begins his resume with a profile section that summarizes his achievements in sales. I must admit to sometimes ignoring a career summary or profile and proceeding directly to the experience section. In this case, however, the profile section is relatively brief, provides details and examples, and sticks to the candidate's real achievements in the sales profession, so it works.

- Often, in professions such as sales where education may not be a primary factor in an individual's capabilities and/or chance for success, education may be listed near the end of the resume. A college degree should always be noted on the resume.

- Career path is clearly visible with position titles and company names underlined and upper case, respectively. Dates are easily discerned.

- Bulleted points highlight actual achievements and/or areas of expertise rather than just summarizing each position. Johann provides many detailed examples, including numbers, always a good thing in a sales resume.

- A resume must always account for every year of a candidate's career from beginning to the present. Johann provides detailed descriptions of the last 15 years of his 23-year career, which happen to coincide with all of his experience in medical and/or hospital related sales. He appropriately lists his prior, unrelated experience selling for a foundry and an oil company in a single paragraph, without providing unnecessary details from his early, unrelated positions.

- A short description relating the size and breadth of each employer would be a good addition to this resume.

Sample Resume #3 (Good): The Recent College Graduate

Anne Wilson
Insert contact information here

EDUCATION:

Marquette University, Milwaukee, Wisconsin
College of Communication, August 2004 –December 2007
BA in Advertising; Graduated in 3.5 years

PROFESSIONAL EXPERIENCE:

QQQ Capital Ventures, Winter Park, FL and Naperville, IL
Consulting Assistant, May 2008 – Present
  Highlights:
- Researched Class of Trade and Channel of Distribution issues in pharmaceutical sales.
- Conducted survey research with industry thought leaders.
- Contributed to the writing of a white paper for presentation to a large healthcare company.

O'Riley-Duff Public Relations, Milwaukee, WI
Public Relations Intern, January 2008 – May 2008
  Highlights:
- Wrote by-lined articles for healthcare and engineering trade publications.
- Procured national and local coverage for Major Player, Inc.
- Created database for media tracking.
- Joined ABC and XYZ accounts in addition to primary account, Major Player, Inc.
  Daily responsibilities: tracking media coverage; writing and editing by-lined articles for trade publications; assisting in crisis communication materials; preparing national and international conference proposals; pitching editorial content and news releases; compiling media lists, writing and distributing media alerts; creating news release database.

2MyHealth, LTD, Dallas, TX
Marketing Intern, May 2007 – August 2007
  Highlights:
- Created four interactive patient education programs.
- Designed media materials.
  Daily responsibilities: researching medical conditions; writing script for videos; designing patient education disks and packages; compiling data on national HMO and PPO plans; researching outdoor advertising.

Schneider-Schmidt Advertising and Public Relations, Milwaukee, WI
Floor Intern, August 2006 – December 2006
  Highlights:
- Created mock radio buy with Media Planners.
  Daily responsibilities: transcribing interviews with physicians; monitoring media, proofreading and editing, assisting with administrative duties.

Family Doings Magazine, Oak Park, IL
Advertising and Sales Intern, May 2005 – August 2005
  Highlights:
- Wrote and designed monthly flyers based on editorial calendar.
  Daily Responsibilities: compiling and sending media kits; contacting national corporations to create relationships; distributing flyers locally.

Notes on Sample Resume #3

Anne Wilson is a recent college graduate who used the above resume format to successfully land her first real job as a marketing assistant at a Chicago-based firm. Her resume, like the previous two samples, is attractive, readable and clear.

For a recent college graduate without a long list of employers, confining the resume to one page is a goal, unless doing so sacrifices valuable content.

- On a short resume, a variety of formats will create a clear, concise look.
- The goal of a resume is to sell your potential. As one of many college graduates in a sluggish economy, Anne differentiated herself from her fellow graduates by emphasizing her early graduation and her internships. Other college graduates may have different achievements and attributes they can emphasize to stand out from the crowd. Outstanding GPA, success on an athletic team, membership in volunteer or professional organizations are among these. Present every job as a learning experience. Emphasize leadership or accomplishments.
- Because all of her work experience consisted of short-term internships, no lengthy descriptions were necessary. Bulleted lists of achievements worked very well.
- A brief description of each employer would be a helpful addition to this resume.

Sample Resume #4 (Not-So-Good): The Run-On Resume
(See next page)

JESSICA NEWKIRK
(Insert contact information here)

CAREER OBJECTIVE: To obtain an executive leadership position that furthers my career in the marketing field.

PROFESSIONAL EXPERIENCE:
BEST ELEVATOR, CO, "Every Elevator Our Best Elevator"
Green Lake, Oklahoma *SENIOR MANAGER, PRODUCT DEVELOPMENT& MARKETING, Apartment Solutions (2005 to present.)* Responsibilities include: direct and manage the "Apartment Building Solutions" team in a $400 million dollar market. Development and execution of strategic business plans to grow sales in targeted market and brand segments worldwide. Lead strategic business initiatives and innovative approaches utilizing the "Listen to the Developer" process in order to expand into new applications, platforms and markets. Conduct consumer insight research, construct competitive intelligence and analysis, build brand marketing and brand awareness strategies across all platforms. Cross-functional leadership in the creation and strategic development of innovation projects that are focused on revenue and earnings growth, including working with internal Design, Marketing & Engineering Organizations and the development of key external partnerships to identify business opportunities and development priorities. Accountable for executive reporting and the presentation of the Metropolitan Apartment Building Solutions Pipeline results.

NICE FIXTURES CO., "Made-to-Order Bath Environments" Manufacturer of products for bathrooms. *Pleasant Park, Missouri. SENIOR MANAGER, BUSINESS DEVELOPMENT, Emerging Markets (2001 to 2005.)* Accountable to pursue and deliver strategic opportunities for growth through partnerships. As the Business Development Sr. Manager, contributions included: identifying, exploring, and executing opportunities that either enhanced or expanded the core of the business. Specific performance measurements included: customer, market & trend research, the development of strategic business models & tools for new business and emerging markets, creating a diverse network of strategic partnerships through contracts, alliances and /or acquisition activities. When applicable, the orchestration & management of pilot concepts with target customers / partners as a proof of concept prior to commercialization; also worked closely with key constituents and the executive team to demonstrate, support, and encourage an innovative mindset inside the corporation.

Bird Creek, Missouri 2000. SENIOR MANAGER, Marketing Communications & Ebusiness. A senior level strategist and business development role serving key internal & external constituents as a member of the Senior Leadership Team for start-up ebusiness unit. Developed and led the Integration B2B strategy for key corporate clients, dealers and internal partners. In addition, accountable for the recruitment, training, marketing communications and management of a North American team of diverse professionals, this team was accountable for the development, implementation, and services of best-in-class B2B customized websites that provided a direct connectivity for sales & marketing between Nice Fixtures, the dealer and prospective or existing customers. This business unit and B2B website sales & marketing tool continue to be a strategic competitive advantage to the corporation.

etc.etc.etc. (edited for space purposes)

EDUCATION AND: AWARDS:	• Nice Fixture Co. Innovation Award '96 • University of Missouri-MBA-'04 • Workplace Safety Certification- '91	• Nice Fixture Co. Leadership Award '92 • Mercy College BA -Education-1990 • Student Congressional Internship-'1988
PROFESSIONAL ASSOCIATIONS:	• PDMA: Active Member • The FWO: Past Member • Saint Mary Hospital Volunteer • Bird Creek Library Council Member	• Leadership Network: Active Member • PTA: Past Associate Member • Mercy College Alumni Club • Bird Creek Humane Society Volunteer

Notes on Sample Resume #4:

Did you notice that Ms. Newkirk has an attractive background, having worked her way up from her modest beginning as an entry-level administrative assistant with a teaching degree to her current position as a qualified product development/marketing professional with an MBA? If you managed to discover that information, you scrutinized the resume very closely.

Unfortunately, many potential employers (and recruiters) probably did not don reading glasses and squint to discover the MBA, and this woman's accompanying record of success. She will not attract the attention she deserves without some major resume reconstruction.

- Jessica has used small type, long paragraphs, and little or no open space. The result is a jammed-in, run-on resume that is hard to examine at a glance. Increasing the font size and adding some blank lines would increase readability.
- The dates of employment and position titles are hidden within bodies of type. Dates and titles should be clearly visible.
- Extensive mixing of fonts, italics, bold-face, parentheses etc., makes this resume visually unattractive.
- Use of bullets would provide emphasis. The lengthy descriptions in this resume should be shortened, particularly regarding early positions.
- This resume includes a "Career Objective." I generally deem this unnecessary unless a candidate wishers to veer in a different career direction than the obvious. Most employers will understand that an individual wants to move a step forward in his or her career.
- The candidate's recent MBA from a well-known school is hidden at the end of the resume among such items as her 20-year old Workplace Safety Certification. Education warrants a separate category. Because her MBA is a recent and important achievement, the candidate should have presented it at the beginning of the resume.

- Many memberships and awards are irrelevant to a potential employer and should not be listed. Exceptions: If you are a recent graduate without much work experience, or vying for a sales-type position and trying to demonstrate your contacts in a community, listing of memberships might be important. Otherwise, limit memberships to those in which you have held major positions, or those that indicate that you are held in high professional esteem by your peers or have made significant achievements in your profession.

---USE OF EXECUTIVE SUMMARIES---

One resume element that has an equal number of proponents and detractors is the Executive Summary, sometimes included near the beginning of the resume. Some feel the summary is a waste of white space on the document. Others feel that it is a very useful component of a complete resume.

If an individual has a lengthy career (in excess of fifteen years), I think a summary can be effective in focusing the reader's attention on what is important. That being said, it should be very brief and highlight key strengths that the individual wants considered. A long summary is an oxymoron (large shrimp) and sets a bad tone for the remainder of the resume.

---QUICK TIPS FOR RESUMES---

For more extensive help, conduct an internet search using the term "resume writing." You will find an abundance of information from a variety of sources. Some of the "rules" you discover might conflict with others. This is because few hard, fast rules actually exist. Having said that, here are some of my own "rules" and personal preferences.

Headhunter Bob's "YES!" List:

- Name and contact information in large and/or bold type at the beginning of the resume.
- Typeface of at least 11-point.
- Consistency of format - If you capitalize a word or term at the beginning of the resume, make sure you capitalize it throughout. Use of boldface, upper case, italics, bullets, punctuation, etc. should be consistent from the beginning to the end of the resume.
- Proofreading – Absolutely no mistakes allowed.
- Dates that are easy to see at a glance - Include dates of academic degrees, which will be verified at some point.
- Inclusion of all information – Do not hide or exclude any position or military service from the beginning of your career to the present. If your resume is getting long (over 3 pages), list and/or summarize your earliest few jobs in a paragraph designated "Early Career Experience."
- Separate sections for education and career experience.
- Career experience in reverse chronological order from most recent to earliest.
- Present tense for your current position; past tense for previous positions.
- A separate section for important qualifications including certifications and technology skills, if applicable to the position at hand.
- Visual emphasis (Bold or Uppercase) on company names and your title at each company.
- Descriptions of each employer's size, location and industry.
- Brevity – Being brief forces the writer to focus on the important, rather than the superfluous. It is especially important to be brief when providing descriptions of positions more than ten years in the past.
- Important details – Shorter is better, but don't be stingy with details. That special project you worked on for nine months might be the singular most important factor in qualifying you for your next job.

- Tailoring of information to each recipient – Desktop publishing allows you to make slight adjustments of emphasis based on the specific position you are pursuing.
- White space – Blank lines between bodies of text make a resume more readable.
- Bullets – Use bullets if a body of text is more than five or six lines long.
- Reason for job change (sometimes) - If you have made an unusual number of job changes that might raise an employer's eyebrows, it may be helpful to explain on your resume that your company closed, went bankrupt, was sold, etc. If the reasons for change reflect negatively on you, do not include them.

Headhunter Bob's "NO!" List:

- Lies – Never lie on a resume. This is one of the few sure-fire ways to destroy your career. As a headhunter, I verify such items as degrees and professional certifications and in many cases check references with former employers. If you are lying, it will be discovered by me or by your prospective employer. Once it has been discovered, you will be fortunate if you are ever able to re-establish the career you had.
- Omissions – Just like lies, any omissions you make in a resume are considered deceptive and will eventually be discovered. For instance, do not try to fudge on your age by omitting the first 15 years of your career or the dates of your degrees or initial employment. A potential employer will discover and resent your effort to hide important facts about your background.
- Self-descriptive adjectives – If you regard yourself as "high-energy" or "hard-working" or "cheerful," that is super, great, and excellent. But an employer will judge for himself, based on your interview and your track record.
- Job descriptions that say nothing – You must provide details of what you did, especially when seeking high-level jobs.

- Typos.
- Very small (9-pt. or less) typefaces.
- Mixing of any more than two typefaces.
- Extended bodies of typed copy with no visual breaks. Utilize bullets or white space.
- Unimportant information – like memberships, hobbies, etc. that are not directly related to your career.
- "References Available" line – unnecessary. The employer will ask for references if desired with or without inclusion of this line on your resume.

---THE COVER LETTER---

After you have completed a working resume, you are almost ready to send it out to targeted companies. Almost! Unfortunately, for those of you who detest writing, each resume you send out must be accompanied by a cover letter, briefly explaining the reason for the correspondence. Resumes not accompanied by cover letters may create confusion in the minds of recipients as to why you have submitted a resume at this particular time.

For a wealth of information on writing cover letters, I suggest doing an internet search using the term "writing cover letters." You will find advice and many sample letters. Here, as you might expect, are a few suggestions from me:

- Print your cover letter on the same stationary as your resume, preferably white. Obviously, if you are sending an e-mail, this doesn't apply.
- Include your name and contact information in a letterhead at the top of your cover letter.
- If you are sending your cover letter and resume via e-mail, embed the resume in the e-mail, in addition to attaching a separate file for printing

purposes. As a headhunter in a hurry, I am often more likely to peruse a resume if I don't have to open an attachment.

- A cover letter should be no longer than one page. Think of it as an appetizer preceding the resume, which is the dinner portion. Do not recite your entire resume in the cover letter.
- The first paragraph should explain why you are submitting your resume to the company or recruiter. If you are responding to an ad for a specific position, name the position and reference where you encountered the advertisement. If not, name a position title or level you are seeking.
- If at all possible, make use of "hooks". If you make reference to the name of someone the reader knows, the odds that your letter/resume will be reviewed increase dramatically. For example, your opening sentence may look like this: "At the suggestion of Bob Ward, your Vice President of Marketing, I am submitting my resume for your consideration." If a current employee is referenced, it causes the reader to give your information more attention.
- Following the introductory paragraph, include several paragraphs highlighting one or two important elements of your background. These may include academic degrees, professional certifications, most recent position, or a notable accomplishment. Again, do not recite your entire resume in your cover letter.
- Tailor your letter to the position you are seeking.
- Proofread for grammatical errors and/or typos. An error in your cover letter is fatal.
- Close the letter with a brief paragraph thanking the potential employer for his or her time and consideration.

One final note: When you are composing your cover letter, always be straightforward and cognizant of your reader's time and patience. The following two cover letter lead-ins are examples of people who weren't.

"Imagine the courage of George Washington as he led his half-frozen troops across the ice-encrusted Delaware in 1776..."

"Imagine the appeal of Cats, a long-playing Broadway musical that appealed to the masses without generational boundaries..."

I ***magine a headhunter*** *who quickly loses interest in trying to figure out whether the above two messages were from CFO candidates, long- term life insurance salesmen, or Spam Central Station. These represent real-life examples of e-mails and or letters I have received from potential candidates. Each piece goes on (and on) for several paragraphs before getting to the point of the message, which is "I am looking for a job."*

If you are trying to attract a recruiter's or employer's attention, it is much more effective to be concise and direct in your communications, than it is to showcase your recent creative writing class. Be considerate of your recipient's time if you are hoping for positive, not negative, attention.

---SUMMARY---

If I can emphasize only one thing about writing a resume, it is *"Do it now!"* Chances are, it won't be nearly as difficult as you think. One thing is certain. The task will not become any easier tomorrow or next week or next month. Without a resume, you can not progress in your career because you will not be invited to interview for a position.

When you begin composing your resume, start with your most recent position, and then work your way backward. Refer to past resumes to prompt your memory of long-departed positions, dates of employment, dates of academic degrees, and other details. Use the guidelines and format suggestions I have provided, as well as research from online or published resume building sites.

When you have finished your first draft, show it to a spouse, a parent, a sibling, or a trusted friend, and request his or her honest input. In this day of word processing, changes and revisions are easy, and resumes can be cut and pasted to customize for specific positions.

Once you have composed a resume, you are prepared to respond whenever an opportunity presents itself. Or, if you are currently engaged in a job search, you are ready to begin sending out your marketing piece to targeted recipients. A good resume is the first step in that process.

INTERVIEW MASTER

Interviewer:

You have a very nice resume. It stood out among the other resumes that we received because it was so easy to read and it highlighted the environment and experience that overlaps our needs nicely.

Candidate:

I have known about your company and have had an interest in working here for several years. I look forward to discussing the specifics of the position with you.

Chapter 4

Research and Networking:
Spreading your Wings and your Resumes

INTERVIEW DISASTER

Interviewer:
I see you have been unemployed for six months. This position has been posted for three months. I wish we would have heard from you sooner.

Candidate:
I had a severance package, so I decided to delay my job search and accomplish a few household projects. First there was the basement, then the attic, then painting the living room. When I finally finished putting all my vacation pictures into photo albums, I decided it was time to look seriously for a new position

---

You have now committed to making a job change and gone to the effort of designing an attractive, well-organized resume. You regard your resume with great satisfaction and think, *"Who wouldn't want to hire someone like me?"*

Your resume may be eye-catching, but it will not catch anyone's eye while it is resting comfortably in a Word file on your computer or gathering dust on the corner of your desk.

So where are you going to send this masterpiece of self-promotion? Without even thinking you may be able to name three or four or even ten companies in your industry, but in a challenging economy, three or four or ten may not be enough. Seventy-three may not be enough. No amount of resumes is enough until you are placing a picture of your beloved pet (or family member) on your new desk.

Putting yourself "out there" in the job marketplace calls for patience and fortitude. It will require assistance from your friends. It may require some learning if you have not mastered using the internet, and some guts if you are not comfortable initiating cold calls. If good fortune comes your way, your search will be short. If not, your search will demand time, resourcefulness and perseverance. But with some hard work and some knowledge of research and networking, your project will be rewarded with a satisfying new position.

Research and networking can be divided into three major categories:

- Traditional personal networking
- Published and/or online networking,
- Recruiters

An effective job search will probably include all three options.

---TRADITIONAL PERSONAL NETWORKING---

By far, the most productive method of marketing yourself is personal networking. In the minds of many people, it is also the most difficult. At a time when the natural inclination may be to wrap yourself in a cocoon of privacy, the correct action is to spread your wings and be noticed.

As unlikely as it may seem, each person you know is a potential source of valuable information; from your niece's husband to the parent of your daughter's soccer buddy to your barber. Make an all-inclusive list of your contacts, no matter how distant the relationship. Reach out to each one either formally or informally, and make it known that you are in the process of making a change.

I like to play the guitar. I LOVE to play my guitar with others who share my interest in music. On many Sunday afternoons, I host an informal get-together of "musicians" who will happily play for beer. On one of these occasions, we were joined by a young man from my neighborhood, a new acquaintance. Unbeknownst to me, this young man was a recent college graduate looking for an entry level position in finance. Unbeknownst to him, I am a headhunter. By the end of our guitar session, I had requested a copy of his resume. A day later, I contacted a friend and long-time business associate, who happily agreed to take a look at the resume. Within a week, an interview had been scheduled. Within three weeks, the company had hired the young man. Jam session to job: one never knows the path to a regular paycheck.

Keep in mind that each person on your contact list probably knows about 100 people. So a good, productive contact with ten people has the potential to multiply your reach to nearly 1000 individuals. That's how networking works.

When you reach out, a one-on-one conversation with a contact is generally more effective than a written communication. If you summon the courage to call someone, he or she will be forced to put some thought into your request, whereas an e-mail message can be read and ignored.

If the idea of initiating networking phone calls makes you nervous, you are in good company. Nevertheless, you must overcome your anxiety and make the calls if you are to reap the rewards of networking. To make yourself more comfortable, it is best to prepare in advance. Script what you are going to say. Recite your presentation multiple times so that you can deliver the words smoothly. Practice it several times and even record yourself so that you know how it sounds. (Believe it or not, all this rehearsing actually will make you sound more natural!)

When you are speaking to a possible resource, be brief, factual and to the point. Explain that you are in the process of looking for a new job. Succinctly focus on what you have been doing, what you want to do, where you want to do it, and possibly provide some idea of your salary requirements. Ask if your contact can help you with any information about companies or opportunities within your target industry. Ask if he or she knows anyone who might be seeking a candidate with your qualifications. If so, request a referral to a person of interest.

You may want to check your ego at the door when you undertake this process. Many of your "friends" may not give you the time of day. But the more people you contact, the greater your chance of identifying an opportunity. This is not baseball where you have to worry about a batting average. All you need is ONE hit.

Sales expert Zig Ziglar once said: *"Timid salesmen have skinny kids."* [1] I want your kids to be fat and happy. Forcing yourself to execute a personal networking strategy may be challenging, but it will maximize your odds of finding a job and keeping the spaghetti on the table.

---PUBLISHED AND/OR ONLINE NETWORKING---

When you are looking for new employment, you will need to learn about and avail yourself of the many published and online resources available to the job seeker. This topic could fill many a book, but since the actual job interview is the focus of this book, I will only cover some of the most easily accessible resources.

Job Posting Sites

One of the easiest and quickest ways to access available positions in your geographic area is visiting an online job posting site. In today's job market, online job posting sites have virtually replaced the large classified jobs section of the newspaper. If you have not previously had a reason to become proficient with the internet, you have one now. If you do not own a computer, make use of your local library and ask for any assistance you need to use the internet effectively.

Online job posting sites such as *CareerBuilder.com, Monster.com, TheLadders.com* and many, many others are easily accessible from your home computer or your local library. At these sites, companies and search firms pay a fee to post their job openings. You can access the jobs at no expense using parameters such as key words, locations, salary requirements, job title, etc. Usually, a job posting will include a very detailed position description, including salary information and contact information. You may be able to e-mail or fax a resume directly through the website.

Higher level positions are often conspicuously absent from the general job posting websites, although more specialized sites now target higher income professionals.

Remember, these job posting sites are free for you to browse. There is absolutely no reason to exclude them from your research, no matter how effective or ineffective you believe them to be. Avoid any job posting site that requires a fee to browse.

Social Networking on the Internet

Social networks have flourished on the internet in the last five years. Millions of people have freely provided information regarding their backgrounds and their current employment status, presumably to make themselves available for social and professional opportunities that might come their way. As a side effect, this has made these people available to you as you conduct your job search.

> *Check what information about you is in the public domain through the internet. Perform a search using your name. Companies can learn about you from many sources including social networking sites, online directories, and blogs. Make sure that the messages circulating about you are the messages you want to circulate. As long as you have never done anything unethical, immoral, illegal or stupid, you needn't worry. Say with me, Uh-oh.*

If you have never used social networking of any kind, you are not alone. Social networking is a relatively new phenomenon brought to us "mature" folks by our sons and daughters in high school and college. Do not be afraid to venture into social networking for the first time. Many sites are user-friendly and provide detailed instructions regarding how to join and use the network. If you are slightly techno-phobic, this may appear to be a daunting task. Ask for help from a friend or just muddle your way through it. If a high school kid can figure it out, so can you.

One of the most well-known business/professional networking sites is *LinkedIn.com*, which has rocketed to the top among the professional ranks. Other online networking sites include *MySpace.com*, *Facebook.com*, *Spoke.com*, and *Plaxo.com*, among others. Each of these networking sites works differently. Some of these sites are more social in nature, some more focused on professional networking. Many are free. Some require subscriptions. They have become respected tools for internal and external recruiters. A brief visit to any of these websites will tell you whether that particular social network can serve your purposes.

Many employers and recruiters use *LinkedIn.com* as a source of candidates. Posting your resume or background information on a network such as *LinkedIn.com* can dramatically raise the possibility of being contacted regarding an opportunity. I suggest providing as much information as you can regarding your career, while maintaining personal privacy. I am much more likely to contact someone who has posted a detailed resume than an individual who has shared minimal information about his or her career.

Candidates can also use *LinkedIn.com* as a source of contacts at their targeted companies. By entering key words, geographic locations, or company names, a candidate may be able to find and connect with individuals who can be a source of jobs, referrals, or information. Many college alums have developed sub-groups to focus networking activity to fellow alums.

Business Databases – Your Local Library

Even if you have not had a library card since the sixth grade, the time has come to re-acquaint yourself with this free resource. Most public libraries provide an abundance of business and career information in their reference areas or through their websites.

Specifically, there are dozens of research companies that gather data on companies and publish the results of their research. Your library may subscribe to one or more of these services and offer access to cardholders free of charge. These business databases provide information on thousands of companies, including financial data; size based on employee count or revenues; headquarters and subsidiary locations; and often the names of key individuals in the company.

So conquer your library-phobia and pay a visit to your local library. Approach the reference librarian (she's that friendly looking woman sitting at the big desk that says "Reference Materials") and tell her you are interested in accessing the library's business databases as part of your job search. The librarian can lead you to published resources and walk you through them. Better yet, she can lead you to one of the library's computers and teach you to access similar information online.

Utilizing online business databases may seem overwhelming at first, but with some initial assistance from the reference librarian and a little learning time, the process is very manageable. Once you learn to use these online resources at the library, you can often utilize that knowledge at your home computer with only a library card/account to sign in.

Do not be afraid to ask questions. It has been my experience that librarians are eager to help you. I suspect you will be amazed at the amount of information that can be gained from the local library. And who knows - you might even find a suspense thriller that will add some excitement to your days of unemployment.

*W*hen my daughter *was seeking her first post-college employment with a new advertising degree, my wife and I pointed her to Reference USA, an online database accessible through our library cards. Using our home computers, we were able to pinpoint a targeted list of mid-sized to large companies located in the Chicago Loop.*

Cherry-picking companies in professions that interested her, she was able to learn each company's location, mailing address, size, number of employees and often the name of an executive within the firm such as the Human Resources Executive or the Marketing Coordinator. Using the information she acquired, my daughter was able to submit resumes to these executives by name via mail or e-mail. Within two months, in a terrible economy, she had interviewed at several of these companies and acquired a job as a marketing assistant in a prestigious law firm.

Associations and Groups

Professional associations and college alumni groups often have career services and/or job posting and resume posting sites. Take advantage of any active groups you are eligible to join which provide these services. Post your resume and search career postings. You may have to shell out a small annual dues payment to join.

---RECRUITERS---

Recruiters and/or executive search firms may well have a place in your networking efforts. In order to find and utilize this resource, you must know a little bit more about the recruitment business than you probably know now. Your friendly headhunter comes to the rescue yet again.

First, it should be understood that recruiting firms are responsible for a very small percentage of all jobs filled and should not be used as your sole method of networking. This is because recruiters are paid by employers, and employers will not choose to pay a fee if they believe they can fill a position on their own.

*R*ecently, *a neighbor stopped me on the sidewalk to ask me if I could help her unemployed son find a job. It would be impossible for even a former bean counter like me to calculate the number of friends, acquaintances, business associates, and family members who have approached me over the years with similar requests. While I am flattered to be viewed as a benevolent Santa Claus who can deliver great positions to all deserving job-seekers, honesty demands that I correct their misconceptions and inform them that this is not how my business works. As a retained recruiter, I am hired by a company to hunt for a highly specialized person to fill a specific position (hence the term headhunter). So, though I would love to be able to find jobs for friends, family members, friends of family, and families of friends, and I am certainly happy to accept a resume and keep it on file, it is only rarely that an unsolicited resume landing in my hands happens to match one of the positions that I have been assigned to fill. (Merry Christmas to all!) Too often, I can only deliver a lump of coal.*

Although recruiting firms are not in the business of finding jobs for individuals, a good search firm can be helpful to a job-seeker in many cases. If a recruiter contacts you about a position, you are well-advised to listen. While in the job market, it can also be helpful to initiate contact with a recruiter, while continuing to pursue other job hunting avenues on your own.

In addition to firms such as mine that are assigned to fill permanent positions, a number of firms deal only with temporary or contract assignments.

Temporary Placement Firms

Temporary or temp firms usually work on hourly opportunities ranging from labor to administrative to short-term professional roles. The temp firm receives an order from a client for one or more specified individuals and is expected to produce such individual(s) on very short notice. Therefore, the temp firm must necessarily have an "inventory" of individuals who would be possible fits for the type of openings they address.

If you are in a struggling industry and/or see little chance of permanent employment in the near future, you might consider providing your resume to a temp firm. A temporary assignment will bring in a salary as you continue to seek permanent employment and possibly provide a bridge to a new industry. Be very careful that you do not devote all your energies to the temporary assignment and lose track of your goal to find a permanent position.

Permanent Search Firms

As explained above, companies hire search firms to find specific individuals for specific roles. This is the only way a reputable firm works. A JOB SEEKER SHOULD NEVER PAY A FEE TO A RECRUITER.

Here is some other information to consider before entering into a relationship with a recruiter:

- If you are employed and worried about confidentiality, you should tread carefully into a relationship with any recruitment firm, as the firm may actively market a good resume to a number of companies, hoping to make a match. If you are not careful, your resume may find itself in the hands of your current employer (who has not yet told you you're fired). Tell the firm that you expect confidentiality and insist that the recruiter receive your permission before sending your resume to any company. It is advisable to know that a firm is reputable before entrusting that firm with your personal information.
- Avoid supplying your resume to TOO many search firms, as a potential employer may receive your resume from multiple sources, resulting in confusion and possible fee disputes. Most employers are hassle-averse and will simply eliminate you from consideration rather than cope with potential conflict.
- Many companies retain search firms to fill their high level positions. These firms may provide your one and only entry point into positions such as these. So do not hesitate to contact a search/recruitment firm to inquire about current opportunities, recognizing that none of those opportunities may match your credentials.
- Some retained firms specialize in very specific areas such as finance or information technology. If you find a firm that specializes in your particular field, by all means, make sure that firm has your resume.
- Just as there are knuckleheads in the ranks of electricians, lawyers, retailers and doctors, there are unprofessional recruiters. Use your intuition when establishing a relationship with a recruiter, keeping in mind that an unprofessional or unethical recruiter may be a sign of an unprofessional or unethical client.

Using Search Firms

By submitting your resume to search firms, you are furthering the goal of networking and making yourself more "findable" to an employer. It is important to associate yourself with reputable, experienced firms that have some track record working with companies in your profession.

---SUMMARY---

As a general rule, more is better when deciding what avenues to pursue en route to your new position. The more research you do, the more people you contact, the more resumes you send out or post online, the more search firms you call or e-mail, the better your chance of success in your job search.

If you have contacted a dozen recruiters, sent resumes to a hundred firms and posted your resume on every job networking site you can find, keep contacting, sending and posting. Your job search is not done until your new job is won.

INTERVIEW MASTER

Interviewer:

I went to college with your aunt, and then worked with her for several years at EfCo. We've remained in contact ever since then. I'm so glad you let her know that you are available to interview for our sales position.

Chapter 5

The First Pitch:
Surviving your Initial Screening
by Phone or E-mail

INTERVIEW DISASTER

Outgoing message – Voice mail of job candidate Michael Murphy
Dude, you have reached the voice mail of Crazy Mike. If it's Tuesday or
Thursday, I'm at a bar crawl. If it's Wednesday or Friday, I'm recovering.
If I'm not picking up the phone, I don't want to talk. Leave a message and
I may or may not get back to you. BEEP.

Once you have sent out your first resume, you must consider yourself "in play" at all times. You will be judged by your professionalism or lack thereof in every contact you have with a potential employer. The first of these contacts will probably be via phone or e-mail. So.....

- Answer your phone with care, even if you're expecting a call from your tequila-shooting college roommate. Assume that you will be judged by your seriousness or your moronic jokes; by your poise and your energy level; by your answering machine message.
- Try to have a resume near the phone so that you can be prepared to discuss your career whenever opportunity calls.

- Make sure your e-mail address appears professional.
- Check your e-mail inbox daily so that you respond promptly to mail sent by a potential employer. Frequently review e-mails that have been automatically directed, incorrectly, to your spam/junk mail file.
- Proofread each e-mail you send out. Assume that you will be judged by your vocabulary, grammar, spelling and punctuation.

Now, let's look at how to deal with your first contact from an interested recruiter or employer via e-mail or phone.

---FIRST CONTACT VIA E-MAIL---

E-mail has become a very acceptable vehicle through which an employer can establish contact with a candidate. It is free, efficient, and can be confidential as long as a personal rather than business e-mail address is used. Using your business office e-mail address to search for a new job is not a brilliant move. Using a frivolous personal e-mail address (sarah38d@yahoo.com) is also not a brilliant move. If necessary, create a new e-mail address for purposes of your job search. It should be personal to you only, straightforward and professional.

From a candidate's perspective, an initial e-mail correspondence from an employer has a definite advantage over an unanticipated phone call, as it gives you some time to do some company-specific research and preparation for an actual conversation.

If you receive an unsolicited job-related e-mail from a company or recruiter, it is likely that a friend or colleague has provided the sender with your contact information. Alternatively, the company might have used a social networking site or your world-famous blog to access your e-mail information. Whatever the source, knowledge of your e-mail address indicates some bit of knowledge about your background and, presumably, can signify a valuable contact.

A job-related e-mail from a company will probably provide you with a position overview and a means of getting in touch. You may be asked to complete an application form attached to the e-mail or at the company's website.

If an e-mail correspondence interests you, you should respond within a day or two. If the company has provided you with a name and phone number, feel free to call that person. Otherwise, you should reply by e-mail and request a convenient time for a telephone conversation. Do not call a company if you have been directed to respond via e-mail. You risk appearing over-eager and possibly antagonizing your contact person at the company. Eager is good. Over-eager is not so good.

Once you have responded to an e-mail message, wait patiently for at least a week before taking any further action. If a week passes from the time of your response to the initial e-mail, you may send a second e-mail, in which you can confirm receipt of your initial correspondence and ask for a status report.

I advise you to respond to all job-related e-mails, even if you decide that a specific position does not interest you. If this is the case, decline in a friendly manner via e-mail, thank the company for its interest, and wish the company luck with its search. Keep the contact information. An individual's business e-mail address is valuable. You never know when you will need a networking outlet.

If an external recruiter has sent you an e-mail, simply respond that you are or are not receptive to further discussion. Even if you decline to be interviewed for a specific position, attach a resume to your response and provide a short description of the type of position you are seeking. Placing your resume in a good recruiter's hands is never a bad thing (said the recruiter to the prey).

Initial contact via e-mail is virtually always followed by a phone call before a face-to-face interview is scheduled.

---FIRST CONTACT VIA PHONE---

Answering the Phone

Any time your phone rings during a job search, the caller at the other end of the line could be the key to your future (or it could be your daughter's long-haired, dope-smoking boyfriend). Answer your home, business, or cell phone in a cheerful, energetic and straightforward fashion, possibly supplying your name (*"Hello, this is Elizabeth Walsh"*). The first words an employer or a recruiter hear from your mouth should not be *"Yo!"* or *"What's up, Dude?"* If you do not have Caller ID, this is a good time to think about getting it.

Your Answering Machine/Voice Mail Message

Your answering machine or voice mail message should perform like a referee in a good sporting event; it should function well and go unnoticed.

Test your answering machine or voice mail to ensure it is working properly. Discovering a call from a potential employer two weeks after the fact may be one week after the job has been filled.

During a job search, your personal answering message should be brief and to-the-point, not a testimonial to your creativity. The first time I encounter a message in song or verse, I may be amused. The second time, I may begin to exhibit symptoms of Impatient Headhunter Disorder. The third time, I may have become frustrated enough to leave an unpleasant (but possibly memorable) message or, worse yet, no message at all. Be respectful of your caller's time and gain his or her respect with a professional-sounding phone message. As soon as a caller hears a recorded message, it becomes apparent that you are not available. Anything beyond a request for a brief message and/or contact information is superfluous.

Omit any profanity, slang and nicknames from your answering machine message. *"Hey, it's Stitch"* may play well with Stitch's friends and family. During a job search, Stitch should replace this message with *"Hello, you have reached the phone of John Schmidt."*

Answering a Random Call at Home

As I said previously, how you answer a random call is important. This applies at the office or at home. If you answer the phone sounding like Attila the Hun, you risk scaring off a potential employer. Even if you *are* Attila the Hun, for the duration of your job search you may want to sound like that affable talk show host on morning TV.

If a radio or television is playing nearby when your phone conversation is taking place, turn off, press MUTE, or move. Why not let your caller envision you composing important documents at your computer instead of watching Jeopardy?

If you have children at home, be sure that they know how to answer the phone properly and take an accurate message. If your children are under ten years old, you may want to keep them from answering the phone until you know the identity of the caller. Much as that Human Resources person loves kids, your one-year-old son's stammered *"hewwo"* may be more amusing to you than it is to a busy professional.

Answering a Random Call at Work

Alternatively, you may receive a call at your place of business. (You control where your calls will be received by the phone number you provide in your resume and correspondence.) A recruiter may call you at your office, but a hiring company most likely will not. A company calling a competitor to directly recruit its personnel is considered bad form (but it is done).

How do you handle job search related phone calls at your place of business? Here are some suggestions:

— **Situation one:**
Your boss and two co-workers are meeting in your cubicle when the phone rings.
Correct response:
DO NOT ANSWER THE PHONE. YOU ARE IN A MEETING, REMEMBER?

— **Situation two:**
You are in a cubicle where every word you say can be overheard by everyone on your floor.
Correct response:
Say that you are busy and would look forward to speaking at a later time. Take the recruiter's number and return the call at your convenience.

— **Situation three:**
You are free to engage in a confidential conversation.
Correct response:
"Yes, I am free to speak to you now. Thanks for calling."

A basic rule of thumb: When you speak to a recruiter or employer, you should be in a relaxed atmosphere where you can think quickly and respond freely to questions. If you are not in such an atmosphere, it is best not to take the call.

Providing your cell phone number is definitely a good option, as long as you answer it when you are in a position to focus on the call, preferably not behind the wheel in heavy traffic.

---THE PHONE INTERVIEW---

Phone interview at 3:00...
It's past 3:00...
I THINK they said 3:00...
DIDN'T they say 3:00?
Today IS Tuesday, right?

Your first extended phone conversation with a recruiter or a company is a delicate balancing act of giving and taking. Your aim must be to: 1) acquire as much information as you can about the company and the role so as to determine your interest level; and at the same time, 2) provide enough information to the recruiter to be recognized as a viable candidate.

A phone interview may be unexpected, or it may be pre-arranged by an e-mail or a brief telephone query that has determined your interest in a position. If you have arranged to be interviewed by phone, prepare yourself for your interview by finding out everything you can about the hiring company through the internet or personal outreach. If your phone interview is unanticipated, you must seek to acquire information about the company and opportunity over the course of your conversation.

> *Warning –Do not underestimate the questions that might come your way during a phone interview. While most phone interviews are casual, they should be treated as The Real Thing…complete with challenging questions. If a phone interview is in your near future, visit Chapter 11 for answers to some tough interview questions.*

Employer Presentation: Questions are your friends!

The recruiter or company representative will probably begin the conversation with a brief presentation about the company and the position. After listening carefully to this presentation, you will get a chance to ask questions or make comments.

I have one bit of advice that will apply to the phone interview and the upcoming chapters on face-to-face interviewing. Whenever you are offered the chance to ask a question, take it. Ask at least one question, maybe even two or three. Asking a question shows that you are attentive, curious, and possibly intelligent. Not asking at least one question makes you look dull and/or uninterested in the opportunity. The only reason not to ask a question is if you have already determined you have no interest in the opportunity.

If this is a pre-scheduled call, your research should have prepared you to ask questions that can help you evaluate the company and the position. Assuming that the recruiter will hit the high points, your questions can be formulated to elicit more details. Consider questions such as:

• How many people are in the department?

- Is the company profitable?
- Is this a branch location or the headquarters?
- Why is the position open?
- Where is the person who was previously in this position?
- What type of technology is in place?
- What is the strategic direction of the department/company?
- What are they trying to accomplish with this position?

Two or three good questions at this point should be adequate to help you determine your initial interest level in this opportunity. If you have decided to move forward, you will have ample opportunity to pose additional questions later at a face-to-face interview.

Candidate Presentation: Hit the high points!

After the recruiter presentation and question/answer follow-up, you will be asked to provide some information about your background and credentials.

If you have already concluded that you have no interest in pursuing the position being discussed, this is the time to terminate the conversation politely without wasting anyone's time. If you extend the conversation, it will be assumed that you have some interest in the opportunity.

Be very careful as you begin to share information about yourself. This is one of several make-or-break points in the process. If you say too much or too little or the wrong thing, you can harm your prospects of success.

Your first task is to determine what the caller already knows about you. Obviously, if the caller has access to your resume, he or she has already deemed that you are generally qualified for the job. In this case, you may want to point out a few impressive highlights of your career from a personal perspective, emphasizing items that might be applicable to the position being discussed.

If your caller has no access to your career information, you will be expected to outline your background, including your current or most recent position, your highest education level, and any important achievements, especially those that might relate well to the responsibilities of this role. The key word here is "outline." You can trust me that a recruiter is not interested in twenty years of detailed professional history over the phone. (Yawn.) Sometimes less is more. Stick to the high points.

Following are two examples of candidate presentations during an initial phone interview. In the first scenario, the candidate is a perfect fit for the opportunity being discussed. In the second example, the candidate is qualified for the position, but her background differs slightly from the stated requirements of the job.

<u>Candidate Presentation Example 1: A Perfect Fit</u>

BIGX Manufacturing Co.'s recruiter has called Joe regarding an opportunity. The position is an outside sales role based in New Jersey, selling to clients in the northeast corridor. The company makes products that are in the same market channel as the product Joe has been selling for several years. The BIGX opportunity would expand Joe's level of responsibility and allow him more input into the sales structure.

The recruiter has described the opportunity. She has explained that she has Joe's resume. She asks Joe to tell her a little about himself.

Here is an example of a good response:

"Since you are familiar with my background, I will try to hit some highlights for your consideration. Based upon your description of the role, there are several interesting similarities within my experience. First, I am very familiar with this particular market space and have been fully engaged in it for over ten years. My track record of success is evidenced by my history of exceeding quota every year for the last ten years.

Second, my home is currently in New Jersey. I have lived in several northeastern states in my lifetime and, therefore, am familiar with the geography and demographics.

Further, I am familiar with BIGX, as I sell products into the same market channel. My industry experience will provide a great foundation upon which to build an expanded knowledge base for the BIGX product line.

While my current role is very similar to the role at BIGX, it appears your opportunity would have several nuances that would be very attractive to me.

What in particular would you like to hear more about?"

Candidate Presentation Example 2: An Imperfect Fit

Do not immediately disqualify yourself from a position based on the stated requirements. If you are close to being qualified, a persuasive presentation can compensate for a few resume deficiencies.

Altering the above example, BIGX is seeking a sales representative who lives in New Jersey with a minimum of ten years of experience selling a product that is very similar to its own. Cara has only six years of experience selling a somewhat different but related product and lives in Ohio. She should not throw in the towel. Instead, she should focus her response on any relevant experience and her record of success.

"You can see on my resume that I have six years of selling products directly into that channel, so I have many contacts in the BIGX market. I have exceeded my quota every year, and, in fact, was twice recognized as the highest producing salesperson of the quarter. I spent the five years prior to that as a product development engineer for SMALLX, your competitor. My engineering background has always been valuable to me, as I can easily understand and explain the intricacies of a product. But my heart has always been in sales. I live in Ohio, but I have

been traveling back and forth to the East Coast every other week for the past five years. Travel is not a problem for me."

Concluding the Phone Interview

If, after your presentation, you have established yourself as a qualified candidate, the recruiter/ company representative may have some more pointed questions to ask you. Listen carefully for the reason behind these questions. Detailed questions may give you some insight as to the key elements of the job, problems related to this position in the past, and the philosophy of management. For example, a question such as, *"Have you ever had a two-year period in which you did not make quota?"* might reveal that the last person in this position had a problem that was not addressed in a timely manner. *"Are you comfortable dealing with the workers in the plant?"* indicates that this will probably be a requirement.

When answering questions, attempt to provide personal examples that will support your capabilities. Your examples should be factual and fairly brief. Long "war" stories with copious amounts of detail, repetition of information, and rambling from the point are likely to lose the listener.

After some discussion of your experience and capabilities, the recruiter will ask you about your interest in the position. Once this happens, you will know that you have succeeded in getting invited to a personal, face-to-face interview.

If the recruiter has not yet mentioned a salary range, it is time for you to do so. There is no point investing time and money in interviewing if the compensation is not attractive. An example of an appropriate salary inquiry is *"The position you have described sounds very interesting to me. Just so no one wastes valuable time on this process, may I ask what the salary range is for this position?"*

In most cases, the recruiter will provide the salary information. If there is a problem with the salary range, say so. Perhaps there is a way to make it attractive. If there isn't, face the facts and be prepared to move on.

If there is no mention of going forward, I suggest that you accept defeat graciously. Keep in mind that it is the recruiter's job to produce qualified candidates, but it does no one any good to pretend that you are qualified for a position. At this point, determine if the recruiter might be able to help you in the future, and try to make the call productive for both parties. If you know someone who might be better qualified for the role, do not hesitate to give a referral. The recruiter will remember you in a positive light when the next position comes along.

---SUMMARY---

This chapter deals with managing your initial e-mail or phone contact from a recruiter or company. Special emphasis is given to the phone interview, which will likely be the first significant exchange of information between you and a potential employer. The phone interview represents a fine balancing act between providing enough information to pique a potential employer's interest and acquiring enough information to determine your interest in the position at hand. If you present yourself well during an introductory phone call, you will maximize your chances of being invited to sit for a face-to-face interview.

INTERVIEW MASTER

Interviewer:
Now that we have spoken and you have outlined some very interesting segments in your career, we would like to speak to you further. Let me ask the obvious question, do you have an interest in pursuing this opportunity?

Candidate:
Absolutely. Your answers to all of my questions have made this position sound like a great fit for me.

I can't figure it out... I always seem to do better on phone interviews than I do face-to-face.

Chapter 6

Interview Strategy:
Thinking Across the Desk

INTERVIEW DISASTER

Interviewer:
Tell me why we should hire you as our marketing director.

Candidate:
Because I've always wanted to be a marketing director...umm, just what exactly does a marketing director do anyway?

Over the years, I have prepped hundreds, if not thousands, of candidates for their interviews. As each interview approaches, I experience a sense of excitement similar to that of a coach sending his team out onto the field of play. As a good coach, I try to emphasize the planned interview strategy, reaffirm my candidate's strengths, and provide a reminder or two that will help the candidate perform to the best of his or her ability.

Of course, each of these prep sessions is unique because each candidate is a unique individual. But no matter the position, the company, or the candidate, one piece of advice remains a constant throughout these sessions: You must make an effort to visualize yourself through the eyes of the other person in the room, that person being your interviewer. I call this "thinking across the desk."

Thinking across the desk means that you do not boast to your interviewer about your speaking skills when she is obviously occupied with her immediate technology problems. It means that you do not tout your remarkable attention to detail when your interviewer desperately needs an innovator. It means that you do not emphasize your people management skills when she is looking for someone who will follow directions from the low end of the totem pole.

*P**icture yourself** walking into an automobile dealership on a Saturday morning, excited about the idea of upgrading your current ride. Upon your entrance, an eager sales associate pops out of his chair, introduces himself and begins the kabuki dance that is known as selling a car. With hardly a word from you, he begins to show you what he has in inventory. You find yourself walking the lot from end to end, looking at the latest and greatest sports cars, several four-door sedans, a convertible, a pick-up truck, and an SUV. None of these models, no matter how shiny, how stylish, or how aggressively priced, is what you have in mind.*

An hour later, you have made no progress. The discouraged salesman hands you his business card. You leave the dealership worn out and dispirited about your chances of getting a new set of wheels.

In spite of your fatigue, you drag yourself to another dealership. Here, a sales associate greets you and invites you to join him in his office. The associate begins asking an organized set of questions to help him determine your likes and dislikes, how you intend to use the automobile, what you like about your current automobile, whether or not you plan to transport children, and your budget limitations.

Given your answers, the associate proposes four or five alternatives and asks for your reaction before taking you around the lot to see the selected vehicles. You begin to assess your desires vs. the cost reality. You begin to analyze what is important in your next vehicle and what luxuries you can live without.

This sales associate has a greater probability of success than the first salesman you encountered because he listened to and analyzed your needs, and showed you only cars that fit your requirements. He focused "across the desk" on you rather than on his own desire to sell a car and earn a commission. By doing so, it just so happens he put himself in a great position to sell you a car and earn a commission.

Before you can begin to think across the desk, you must lose your fear of the person seated across the desk: the intimidating, all-knowing, power-wielding INTERVIEWER.

---THE MYTH OF THE "ALL-KNOWING INTERVIEWER"---

You may have the mistaken impression that every interviewer is a seasoned recruiting professional, trained in the fine art of asking insightful questions and objectively grading each response. Oh yes, her questions seem meaningless and bordering on ridiculous, but you know in your heart of hearts that each is designed to reveal a hidden character flaw or experience deficiency.

Wrong. Some questions are, in fact, meaningless and bordering on ridiculous.

My unscientific observation is that many interviewers, unless they are trained human resource professionals, are as untrained and uncomfortable within the confines of a job interview as most candidates. Your interviewer may be an expert in engineering, marketing, construction, accounting, or banking, but a complete novice when it comes to formulating and asking enlightening questions. In fact, he or she may have only previously experienced interviews from the trembling and quaking position on your side of the desk.

So take some comfort that, while you are feeling intense pressure to provide the perfect answer, your interviewer may be feeling similar pressure trying to generate the perfect question, the magic question that will illuminate the perfect candidate. Based on my experience, the magic question doesn't exist. The magic answer doesn't exist. So try not to place too much importance on any single answer you offer. Your interviewer is a human being. Any mistake you make will be judged by a fellow human being in the context of your total interview performance and demeanor.

---ACHIEVING MUTUAL UNDERSTANDING---

An interview is successful when both parties attempt to address the needs of the other. But in order for that to happen, each of the parties to the interview will first have to discern the other party's motivations and goals.

Your goal, as a candidate, may be escaping unemployment or a bad job, advancing in your chosen career, making more money, achieving personal fulfillment, or re-directing a career path.

> *Your interviewer, on the other hand, has a single motivation: recruiting the best talent in the marketplace capable of solving a specific problem of a company. Recruiting only takes place when workload exceeds capacity or critical expertise is lacking, i.e. when the company needs someone to perform a function that is not currently being performed satisfactorily.*

It is up to you to think across the desk and demonstrate to your interviewer why you are the best person to solve her problem. You must paint a mental picture of how your skills and experience solve the problem that started the recruiting process. Only after this has occurred, will it be up to your interviewer to think across the desk and explain how this position will propel you toward accomplishing your goals.

Many candidates understand this idea in principle, yet have difficulty translating the idea into actual interview dialogue.

I recently counseled a successful professional with about 15 years of experience in the financial field. The man had managed his career well and was seeking a position at the Controller or CFO level. When I asked him what he was looking for in a new position, he replied that he was seeking a position in which he could continue to learn. He emphasized this several times. Finally, I interrupted him with a figurative smack on the wrist. I explained to him that a company which was going to pay a high salary to its next top-level financial person was not the least bit interested in how much that individual could learn, but in how much he already knew. The man looked somewhat dumbstruck. He later confided that my advice was the most breathtakingly simple, yet valuable piece of advice he had ever received relating to a job search.

In a young career, expressing the desire to learn might indicate ambition or drive. But in an established career, 'tis better to ask not what you can learn from your company, but what your knowledge can do for your company.

So how do you tailor your presentation to the needs of your interviewer? How do you begin thinking across the desk?

The best way to become attuned to the needs of your interviewing partner is through questions and answers.

---A TWO-WAY STREET---

Many inexperienced candidates envision an employment interview as maneuvering their way through a rapid-fire barrage of questions. Many hiring managers with limited recruiting experience would be more than happy to be on the delivery end of that barrage. But the result of such a lopsided interview would be an uninformed candidate and a poorly informed manager.

Every good interview will progress from individual presentations of the interviewer and the candidate to back-and-forth discussions of topics most important to each party. The more energy displayed during these two-way discussions, the better the interview is going. Informed questions delivered by energetic participants are indicative of both parties attempting to arrive at a meeting of the minds. If either party seems unenthused about offering or answering questions, it may display a lack of interest or enthusiasm about process.

You should arrive at your interview with a mental or written list of questions you want answered. When you ask your questions, pay careful attention to the responses and especially to the nuances of those responses. The answers you receive will enhance your understanding of the employer's current needs and current situation and give you insight into the thinking of your interviewer. Additionally, the questions you ask will be enlightening to your interviewer.

Only through an open, vigorous question-and-answer session, and careful attention to the answers provided, can both interviewer and candidate achieve a foundation of mutual understanding.

---QUESTIONS AND WHAT THEY REVEAL---

You can listen to an interviewer's questions and provide formulaic answers that you have read in an interview manual and rehearsed in front of a mirror. But it is much more enlightening if you REALLY listen to an interviewer's questions and ponder, *"Hmm, why is she asking that? What is she getting at?"*

If your interviewer has taken the time to prepare meaningful questions for the interview, her questions might be as revealing to you as your answers are to her. Similarly, the questions you ask your interviewer can enlighten her as to your thinking process, your strengths, and your limitations.

Let's look at a few examples of revealing questions.

Revealing Questions from an Interviewer

If an interviewer asks several hypothetical questions about how you would deal with a recalcitrant employee, it might mean that you could find yourself walking into a volatile management situation. If you hate conflict, you might want to ask a few questions of your own before accepting an invitation to a subsequent interview. If, on the other hand, you perceive people management as one of your strong points, these questions give you a clue about what to emphasize in your answers.

If your interviewer's questions repeatedly include technical terms that are well beyond your level of expertise, it is a good bet that you would struggle to meet the technical requirements of the position.

If an interviewer asks about your ability to prioritize work from various sources, it might signal that you will face competing demands from your managers and that this has caused a problem in the past.

Revealing Questions from a Candidate

If your first questions to the interviewer relate to vacation and working hours, she might conclude that you are not particularly ambitious.

If your first questions to the interviewer relate to upward mobility within the company, she might conclude that you are too ambitious (or just ambitious enough).

If your questions include terms that demonstrate familiarity with the technology applications that will be used in this position, your interviewer might gain a sense of comfort with your technical expertise.

If your questions seem too basic for your supposed level of expertise, your readiness for the position may be called into doubt.

Reading Behind the Questions

Do you see how it works? The questions an interviewer asks can shed light on facets of the position that might not be written into the position description. If you listen carefully, chances are you will learn of issues that have been a concern in the past and might become a concern in the future. Knowing these issues can help you to discern whether the position is something you should pursue or avoid at all costs. If you decide to pursue, you can shape your presentation to focus on the issues that underlie the interviewer's questions.

Understand that the reverse is also true. Your questions may expose aspects of your character and personality to the interviewer. It is wise to formulate your questions with this in mind.

<u>Interview Example: Thinking Across the Desk</u>

Cheryl is the Director of Accounting for NewCo, a rapidly growing software company. Over the last two years , day-to-day accounting activity has soared well beyond expectations. The volume of activity has overwhelmed the initial processing methodology and current personnel have been slow to step up to the challenge. Cheryl has a problem and needs a solution in the form of an Accounting Manager with related experience and some new ideas. Cheryl will be most interested in someone who has prior exposure to managing in a similar environment; someone who will bring proven methods to eliminate her problem.

You have received a call from a recruiter regarding the opportunity. Following the call, you accept an invitation to interview at NewCo.

At your interview, Cheryl's initial questions will focus on your ability to perform well based on the requirements of this specific position. She will likely concentrate on your most relevant experience with much less emphasis on any unrelated job history.

For example, Cheryl's questions should focus on prior experience managing day-to-day accounting personnel, IT systems exposure, development of procedures, and change management. If you are listening well, you will immediately begin to visualize the situation and focus your presentation on methodology and management skills, rather than on your three years of selling insurance.

You should ask questions that will clarify the picture. These questions should attempt to clarify the current needs of the company and improve your understanding of those needs. (Save your questions regarding vacation and 401K benefits for the third interview.) If you can see the situation through Cheryl's perspective, it will be much easier for you to propose ideas and outline your solutions.

Once Cheryl has determined that you are a good candidate, she must adjust her focus toward your needs, and strive to make the position attractive to you. Her presentation should include reasons that you might choose to work at NewCo (previously mentioned benefits package), an explanation of how this position might fit into your career path, reassurances about the stability of the company, and other pertinent information to a job seeker.

Based upon the give-and-take of information, you will decide whether you have an interest in the opportunity. Cheryl will decide whether you are the best person to fill the company's needs.

If you have been successful in evaluating and responding to Cheryl's needs, Cheryl will visualize you in the role and begin to address your needs.

---SUMMARY---

The outcome of a successful interview is a candidate with the skills and experience needed to perform the responsibilities of the position matched with a company that can offer a positive environment and attractive compensation package to the candidate. This can only occur if each party to the interview process is able to "read" the other party and even "read between the lines." Listening carefully and formulating your presentation to address the needs of your interviewer rather than your own needs will go a long way toward ensuring your success in the interview process.

By the way, determining that there is a mismatch of these components early in the process is a win for both parties. There are far better ways to waste precious time than with an extensive interview process that has been a no-win situation from the onset. The worst of all worlds is to find a mismatch three months into a new position.

INTERVIEW MASTER

Interviewer:

How would you manage a salesperson who had not achieved quota in two years?

Candidate:

When I was hired as Regional Sales Manager at YouKnowWhoCo, many of the salespeople were underperforming. Within two years, every salesperson was exceeding quota by at least 20%. Here's what I did...

Chapter 7

Interview Attire:
Dressing to Impress

INTERVIEW DISASTER

Interviewer:
The flamenco dancer on your tie is...riveting...and...battery-operated???

Candidate:
I'm glad you like it. My mother gave it to me for my birthday.

As you select the apparel for your next interview, remember one of the basic interview truths described in Chapter 1: A failed first impression is a last impression. With that in mind, consider taking the following brief survey before you leave home.

Wardrobe Reset Survey

⇒ IS ANY ITEM I AM WEARING SOILED, STAINED, SLOPPY, OR SCUFFED?

⇒ IS ANY ITEM I AM WEARING TOO SHORT, TOO LONG, TOO TIGHT OR TOO LOOSE?

⇒ COULD ANY ITEM I AM WEARING BE CLASSIFIED AS "RETRO"?

⇒ COULD ANY COLOR I AM WEARING BE DESCRIBED AS "NEON"?

⇒ DOES MY ATTIRE CALL UNDUE ATTENTION TO ANY PART OF MY BODY OTHER THAN MY BRAIN?

⇒ DOES MY ATTIRE DISPLAY VISIBLE LOGOS?

⇒ DOES ANY ITEM I AM WEARING SHOUT OUT THE HIGH OR LOW PRICE I PAID FOR IT?

⇒ DOES MY CLOTHING MAKE ME LOOK "HOT"?

⇒ DOES A CLOUD OF COLOGNE ANNOUNCE MY PRESENCE IN A ROOM?

⇒ DOES ANY OTHER AROMA ANNOUNCE MY PRESENCE IN A ROOM?

⇒ AM I WEARING "BIG" JEWELRY?

⇒ DOES MY ATTIRE EXPOSE ANY TATOOS OR PIERCINGS OTHER THAN ON MY EARS?

SURVEY RESULTS: If you answered *"yes"* to any of the above questions, press RESET while there is still time.

If your personal style leans toward the trendy, the words classic and conservative may not be part of your vocabulary. Learn them now. When it comes to interviewing, trendy and attention-grabbing are out; boring is in. Dressing to express (your identity, your creativity, your fashion sense) is much different from dressing to impress (your future boss, your future co-worker, The Man).

If you are a man or woman deciding what to wear to your upcoming interview, there are two simple steps you should take:

1. Imagine what you think your interviewer will be wearing; then...
2. Wear a dark suit.

Actually, it's not quite that simple, but almost.

You are probably one of the many people who possess a natural sense of what is appropriate to wear to an interview. But in my years of experience and observation, some who thought they possessed that sense could have been helped by a little independent input. (Friendly headhunter to the rescue!)

Choosing interview attire that is inappropriate, dirty, or wrinkled may indicate poor judgment, a lack of seriousness about the interview, or a lack of professionalism in general. So when a client complains to me about a candidate's interview attire, that complaint is often accompanied by the instruction to terminate the interview process with that candidate. A second chance is rarely given when a first impression has gone awry.

A *former partner* *of mine in the search business had arranged for her male candidate to interview with my client in our offices. She advised her candidate to arrive somewhat early for the interview, to allow time for some last-minute coaching and preparation.*

Right on schedule, the candidate entered our offices, wearing a slinky shirt in a style which only those of us who have survived the disco era would recognize. In an extreme "UH-OH" moment, my partner realized that her candidate (and she...and I) had a big problem. Taking bold, decisive, and, in my mind, gender-specific action, she dragged the candidate to a nearby menswear store, purchased a white dress shirt, had it pressed on the spot, and told the candidate to put it on. (PUT. IT. ON! -- You men with spouses are familiar with the tone.)

The candidate dressed up well and looked the part of a potential high-ranking executive. He ultimately was not chosen for the position, but without my partner's intervention, he would have been dead at "Hello."

I am not a fan of interviews that conclude before a candidate has had a chance to speak. So I am going to provide you with some suggestions on interview attire, encompassing the same advice I give to my candidates before sending them out to interview.

Keep in mind that the following rules regarding interview attire apply to interviews for professional roles. If you are interviewing for a position as a laborer, a store clerk, a teacher's aide, a waitress, a construction worker, a hairdresser, or a similar position, these rules may not be valid. But if the position for which you are applying offers upward professional potential such as promotion to management level, you might want to use these rules as guidelines in any event.

> *A colleague in the recruiting business shared this advice. "Candidates should dress for the job they eventually want to achieve." In other words, dress for where you want to end up in the company, not necessarily where you are now. (This same advice can be applied to how you dress on the job.)*

---BOB'S INTERVIEW ATTIRE RULES FOR MEN---

As I have implied above, the 99.4%-almost-always-correct rule of dressing for a professional job interview is to wear a suit. You may be interviewing in a company that routinely allows casual dress among its employees, but you are not yet working for that company, so have not yet earned the privilege of casual attire at work. It would be a huge mistake to dress casually and discover that your interviewer is wearing a suit, in which case your casual apparel could be considered insulting and unprofessional. Your interviewer has the upper hand here, meaning you are the one who must wear the tie.

Quick Tips for Men

- In most cases, wear a suit. The suit need not be custom-tailored or extremely expensive (unless you are interviewing for the highest-level positions). Avoid the least expensive suit – remember, this is an investment in your future. Your suit should fit well. Your suit coat should close with no problem.
- Your suit should be a dark color, preferably navy, black or gray. Avoid patterns other than very subtle pinstripes.
- Coordinated sport coat, slacks, shirt-and-tie will suffice in some cases.
- A white shirt is the most boring and therefore most acceptable shirt with your suit. A light blue shirt is also acceptable. Cotton and/or cotton blends are the best bet for dress shirts. Avoid contrasting collars, prints and unusual textures.
- All clothing should be freshly laundered or dry-cleaned and pressed.
- Wear a nice-quality, silk tie that complements your suit or sport coat. I happen to be a connoisseur of fine and eclectic ties. However, for a job interview, I might leave my funky, Jerry Garcia tie on the rack and choose stripes or small prints. Most colors are acceptable.
- No logo should be evident on any item of clothing you are wearing. There is no benefit in announcing your wardrobe prices to your interviewer. Leave emblems and embroidered animals at home.
- Your socks should match your suit. Your shoes should be well-constructed dress shoes, polished just before the interview.
- Need I say, a recent shower, fresh deodorant, fresh breath, clean and well-groomed hair and nails are all compulsory. Travel sizes of grooming items can be helpful if you have a long commute to the interview location.
- Carry a briefcase or portfolio in brown or black leather that does not display the logo of a former employer or any other organization. Make sure that this briefcase appears neat when opened, in case you are called upon to produce something from it during the interview.

- Jewelry should be limited to a watch and, if you are married, a wedding ring. Remove the diamond earring. Ditto anything adorning any other facial opening.
- Tattoos should be hidden, if possible.
- Do not wear cologne. Allowing for personal preferences, a subtle scent can be pleasing in a social or personal situation. In a business setting, particularly an interview situation, I recommend avoiding any perfume or cologne.

E *au de Misery…I will never forget an interview I conducted over 20 years ago. It was a typical Chicago summer day with tropical humidity and temperatures in the 90s. At that time, it was the practice of my firm to interview candidates in its small, private offices. Our offices were air conditioned, but on days such as this, the air conditioning had a hard time competing with Mother Nature's supply of humidity. When I walked into one of our small interview rooms to meet my candidate, I nearly doubled over. It was understandable and unavoidable that this young gentleman was glistening, given the heat and humidity of the day, but the combined scent of the candidate and his heavy cologne, confined in this enclosed space, was almost overpowering.*

As we went over his background, I twice made excuses to leave the office to get a breath of unscented air. I was unable to focus on my candidate's resume and his background, only on his abundant cologne. Needless to say, I raced through the interview and did not move this individual forward in the process.

---"BOB'S INTERVIEW ATTIRE RULES FOR WOMEN---

Women are allowed some latitude when choosing interview attire. A woman is allowed to wear a bright colored blouse with her dark suit.

Yes, I am kidding. Actually a woman does have a few more options than a man when dressing for her interview. Call it a double standard, it is important to note here that a woman is not required to look like a man. Femininity is permitted at a job interview, as long as it does not detract from an image of professionalism.

Having said that, for women as well as men, a dark suit is always the best and safest option.

Gee… I felt so good about
myself before the interview…

Quick Tips for Women

- A good quality business suit is the always-safe choice. Black, navy, or gray in solid colors or subtle pinstripes cannot lose.   The suit must fit perfectly with no bulging buttons or pulling fabric.
- Skirt or pants? In my experience, either of these is acceptable. Choose what is most flattering and makes you feel the most confident.
- If you choose to wear a skirt, it should end somewhere within a few inches of your knees. You are interviewing for a professional job, not auditioning for a cheerleading position.
- A coordinated jacket with skirt or pants is also acceptable.
- Under the suit jacket or blazer, wear a sweater, shell, or blouse in a complementary shade. A woman has the luxury of color to underscore

her jacket. Almost anything goes - from royal blue, pink, red, or burgundy, to a more basic gray or silver, ivory, or white. You probably want to avoid neon shades.

- Regarding necklines: Collars, bows, turtlenecks, ruffles, or scooped necklines are acceptable, but anything hinting of cleavage should be avoided.
- A neatly draped scarf is an acceptable color accent.
- Others may disagree, but I think a classic dress can be appropriate and elegant in the interview setting. Select solid colors or subtle patterns; avoid excessive ruffles and frills. Like the skirt, the dress length should be at or near the knee.
- Regarding nylons: I am not a hosiery expert nor do I play one on TV, but here's my opinion. Although nylons have been rejected in recent years by younger professional women, they provide a more finished look to a formal business suit. Much as you may hate them, I suggest that you wear them. An acceptable plan B would be tights.
- Shoes should be heeled pumps with minimal ornamentation. Brightly colored shoes, sandals, and any kind of boots should be avoided. Do not wear a heel higher than you normally wear. Your posture and your walk may be adversely affected.
  (A final note on shoes: I have noticed from raising two daughters that women are rough on shoes. Women's high heels wear out quickly. Keep the heels of your shoes like new, or purchase new shoes for this special occasion. If the toes or any other part of your shoes are scuffed or scratched, polish or replace the shoes.)
- Regarding hair: Again, not an expert. But there are a few general rules that are most often applicable. If your hair is dyed or highlighted, make sure it looks as though it was done professionally, yesterday. Your hair should be shiny, clean, combed, and neat. If wind or rain has mussed your hair, find a restroom and fix it before you enter your interview. Any barrette or hair ornament used to hold back your hair should be as understated as possible. If your hair is bright pink or purple, dye it brown or blonde for the interview.

- Apply your regular make-up conservatively.
- Do not wear perfume (can I say this too much?). Too many people suffer from allergies or simply don't like it.
- Jewelry should look sophisticated, not glitzy and glamorous. A gold or silver chain, a small brooch, a string of pearls or beads, small hoop earrings or studs; you get the picture.
- Other good ideas include; one ring per hand, one earring per ear, one chain or necklace, no jewelry on lips, eyebrows, or nose.

---BOB'S EXCEPTIONS TO THE RULES---

As with any rules, especially mine, there are exceptions.

If you are specifically advised that you may dress casually for an interview, it is acceptable for men to appear in slacks, a golf or polo-style collared shirt without a tie, a sweater and a sport coat; or for women to wear a nice sweater or blouse with business pants or a skirt. All above rules for accessories and grooming still apply.

If you are meeting with someone other than a potential employer, perhaps a friend or colleague who has agreed to talk to you about your job search in an informal setting, business casual dress (see paragraph above) may be appropriate. Keep in mind, though, that casual does not mean sloppy, dirty, old, or unmatched. Casual does not mean jeans. When meeting someone you have not previously met, it is always advisable to wear a suit. The first impression you make on a recruiter or career advisor may determine whether he or she will recommend you to a client or contact.

If you have scheduled an interview during your work day, and your place of business permits casual dress, it may be difficult to wear a suit without raising questions or wry comments among your co-workers. Try to find a way. Other candidates will.

If you are interviewing for a creative position at an advertising agency, architecture, or other creative firm, my advices is to wear a suit unless otherwise instructed, but you may get away with a trendy dress shirt or a quirky tie if you are a man; or trendy accessories if you are a woman.

---SUMMARY---

The all-encompassing rule for selecting interview attire is: your clothing should not detract from attention that should be focused on your qualifications for the job. Three little words come to mind: Conservative; Professional; Suit.

INTERVIEW MASTER

Candidate (to spouse):
Honey, which do you think looks better? The black or the navy suit?

Chapter 8

Interview Formats:
The Resume Review Interview

INTERVIEW DISASTER

Interviewer:

Your resume states that you were responsible for increasing your region's sales at Equipment Corporation by 50% over a three-year period.

Candidate:

REALLY? It says that, huh? Well then, I guess it's true.

Remember long ago when you were in school and a dreaded test date was approaching only too quickly? Invariably, you or a fellow panicky student would raise a hand and ask the teacher whether the upcoming test would consist of essay questions, fill-in-the-blanks, or multiple choice, my personal favorite. Receiving some input as to the test's format gave you and your classmates an idea of how to study and prepare for the test (or not).

So it is no surprise that one of the questions asked of me most frequently by my candidates is *"What will be the format of this interview?"* Because of my knowledge of and/or relationship with the client, I am usually able to provide a pretty accurate answer, possibly including length of the interview, personalities involved, and questions that might be posed.

I have found that even a general outline of what to expect can be a great comfort to a candidate who is facing the great unknown.

There are some fundamental, predictable differences in the methods employers may choose to conduct their interviews. These differences may be determined by chance, by the level or type of position being offered, or by the personal preference of an interviewer.

In my experience, interviews can be loosely divided into three categories. These categories are not mutually exclusive; the lines between them may be blurred and indistinct; and a real-life interview can be a crazy concoction of all three styles. In real life, trying to separate and categorize interview formats can be like trying to separate and categorize the strawberries in a jar of strawberry preserves. Still, the categorization provides us a place to begin our discussion of interview types. So here goes.

After conferring with several colleagues in the search business for input, the three basic interview formats that I will discuss are:

- The Resume Review;
- The Behavioral Interview; and
- The Random Walk

This chapter will be primarily devoted to the first type of interview, the resume review. The next two chapters will deal with behavioral and random walk interviews.

---THE RESUME REVIEW INTERVIEW FORMAT---

The resume review interview format is very commonly used by interviewers, particularly relating to entry level through mid level positions. In the resume review interview, most of the questions an interviewer asks are derived <u>directly</u> from items appearing on the candidate's published resume. The interview sometimes, but not always, follows a chronological path from the beginning of a candidate's career to the end, with emphasis given to past responsibilities or achievements that are relevant to elements of the current position.

Utilizing this interview format, an interviewer would pose very few *"What would you do..."* questions, instead dwelling on *"What did you do..."* questions.

You will know that your interview is a resume review interview when the interviewer peers intently at you resume and begins: *"So, let's take a look at your background,"* or *"Hmmmm....I see that you began your career as an administrative assistant at QRS Company. What were your responsibilities?"* From this point forward, the give-and-take of information will be an effort by you and the interviewer to enhance and build upon the career outline that you have provided in your resume; filling in the blanks with pertinent details.

A resume review interview may consist of a series of direct, specific questions requiring fairly concise, direct answers (Q-A-Q-A style). Alternatively, an interviewer might initiate your portion of the interview with a more open-ended question, such as *"Tell me about your career up to this point,"* or *"Why don't you walk me through your resume?"* later refining her questions to target specific aspects of your background.

---MANAGING YOUR RESUME REVIEW INTERVIEW: ENTRY LEVEL OR SHORT CAREER ---

If your experience portfolio is limited, as is the case with a recent college graduate or a two-year professional, a review of your resume might be expected to kick off about seven minutes of conversation. So, unless you want your interview to end before the half-hour mark has been reached (never a good omen), be prepared to puff up your short resume with interesting bits of information that tend to illustrate your intelligence, work ethic, strength of character, pattern of success, and/or integrity.

You can begin with your academic background, emphasizing your GPA (or not), your major, your alma mater's academic excellence, your reasons for choosing that institution, and the lasting influence it made on you. If you paid your own tuition or worked a demanding job or participated in a sport while attending school, these are points worth mentioning.

If you are a new graduate, you may be able to highlight your achievements over the course of your education, such as part-time employment experience or internships. If you were promoted from a part-time children's swim team assistant during high school to the team's head coach during college, outline the traits that helped you to rise above the rest of the staff. If you ran a successful lawn mowing business with two friends, describe how you marketed your business, performed reliably, mowed in straight lines, set your prices, and collected payments. If you worked in a store, describe how you interacted positively with even the most difficult customers. If you performed an internship during your college days, no matter how menial, be prepared to describe with some detail just how much you learned from all the hours you spent at the copier.

This is not a time to be shy. Sell, baby, sell. Your goal is to provide some insight into your work ethic and thinking process so that the potential employer can connect the dots as to how you may perform in their environment.

Once you have several years of post-education experience, your best interests will be served by focusing your presentation on specific work and/or educational experience that in some way parallels the responsibilities of the current opportunity.

If you are a candidate with a short career history, you will be relieved to know that entry level or lower level interviews generally conclude within about an hour and a half, unless more than one interviewer is involved. If you focus your presentation on what is relevant to the interviewer and are able to provide enough but not too many detailed examples from your background, you have maximized your chances of success. With your mission accomplished, you can still get home for lunch or back to your current job.

Resume Review Example: Matt the three-year engineer

Matt is a mechanical engineer with three years of consulting experience. He is currently interviewing for a staff engineering position in a manufacturing company. Matt finds himself in a resume review interview situation.

After describing the company and the position, the interviewer proceeds to ask questions based on Matt's resume, beginning with Matt's educational background. Matt earned his engineering degree from a respected program. He should be prepared to volunteer information about classes he took and provide some specific examples of the training he received in those classes, projects he completed, and possibly the grades that he earned. If he participated in an engineering internship, he should be able to explain what it entailed. If any of his summer jobs were related to manufacturing and/or engineering, he should find an opening to inject them into the discussion.

The interviewer next advances to Matt's post-college work experience. During his years as an engineering consultant, Matt has worked on several different assignments. Matt should be ready to answer questions about his different clients, and provide detailed explanations of several projects to which he has been assigned and the skills he has learned through those assignments, particularly those which might be transferable to the current opportunity. Matt's presentation will be most effective if it can be summarized with *"I believe my experience with this client/project would serve me very well in the role of staff engineer."*

---MANAGING YOUR RESUME REVIEW INTERVIEW: MIDDLE TO UPPER LEVEL POSITIONS---

If you have an experience portfolio that is longer than ten years, the resume review interview challenge is a bit different. Whereas an entry level or short career candidate might struggle to have enough to say about his single-page resume, a candidate with a 15-year career might struggle to confine his presentation to what is most important, and not litter the playing field with useless information. It is essential to keep the information you provide crisp and interesting to the interviewer and to make it plain how your related experience allows you to solve the needs of the company and the hiring manager (thinking across the desk!).

If your resume review interview is a Q-A-Q-A type, you can expect your interviewer to spend little or no time on the positions you held 15 years ago and delve more deeply into the recent past. Similarly, if you are asked an open-ended question, you will want to fly over the beginning of your resume in order to focus your narrative on more recent, more responsible positions. This flying-over process is commonly referred to as presenting facts from the 20,000-foot level. You can be sure that an interviewer will interrupt and ask for further details when she is interested.

Let me offer an example of an open-ended resume-based narrative based on a 20-plus year career.

Open-Ended Resume Review: Mike the 20-year CFO

Mike is a 42-year-old current CFO who has had three different employers in his career; a public accounting firm and two manufacturing entities. He is currently interviewing for a CFO position at CressCorp, a large manufacturing company.

His interviewer, the VP of Human Resources, has presented an overview of CressCorp and the position in question. With Mike's resume in her hands, she directs Mike to "walk" her through his resume.

Mike, referring frequently to his resume, provides the following response:

"Let me begin at the beginning, but in order to keep this to a reasonable amount of time, I will start out providing detail at the 20,000-foot level and move to ground level as my experience becomes more current. If you wish more detail on anything, feel free to interrupt me.

I was raised in Pennsylvania, the son of a coal miner and a school teacher. My parents instilled a very good work ethic in me, demonstrated by the fact that I have always had a job since I was ten years old.

Throughout high school and college, I worked for Acme Manufacturing. Acme awarded me a full college scholarship, which allowed me to attend the University of Notre Dame, where I earned a bachelors degree in accounting in 1991. I successfully passed the CPA exam in that same year.

My grades in college positioned me to interview with some of the world's best known companies. After investigating several options, I chose to work for BigEight, LLP, a public accounting firm.

I spent three years with BigEight, performing audits of predominantly manufacturing clients such as Caterpillar, Kane Precision Products, and Nabisco. Beyond the recurring audit activity, I gained exposure to several publicly held companies and was involved in registering one company for a public offering.

My experience with BigEight piqued my interest in manufacturing. In 1994, I began to see myself working in that environment versus performing audits. BigEight provided excellent training, a brilliant peer group and great exposure, making it hard to leave. But when I was approached by Kane Precision Products to join the accounting staff, I felt it was the right time and perfect opportunity for me.

Kane is a privately held, tier three manufacturer of components used in large earth moving equipment. Sales approached $50 million, with an employee base of approximately 75. I began as a senior staff accountant in the general accounting area which totaled 6 people. In three years, I was promoted to the General Accounting Manager role.

During my five year tenure with Kane, we converted the accounting system from HiTech software to VeryHiTech software. I led this successful conversion team completing the project well under budget. The completed system allowed us to gather and distribute information on a much timelier basis to the operations personnel.

Additionally, I was a key member of a task force that introduced and implemented lean methodology in several departments. That process was ongoing and beginning to bear fruit when I left Kane in 1999.

At that time, I was approached by The Scheidler Company regarding the role of Controller. The Scheidler Company is also a manufacturing company, but much larger than Kane and with an international presence. Sales at that time were in excess of $300 million. This was a great opportunity for me to take the next step in my career.

At Scheidler, I initially reported to the CFO. My basic responsibilities were to manage the financial reporting process, including the day-to-day accounting duties. I also directed the budgeting and financial analysis function.

My initial challenge at Scheidler was twofold: 1) to evaluate financial personnel and re-staff as necessary and 2) to re-design the process of gathering data, in an effort to develop accurate management information and make it available to stakeholders on a timely basis.

In my first several months at Scheidler, I was able to build a competent staff comprised of some current employees and several additions. My goal was to build a team who was motivated, qualified and accountable. I was able to accomplish that in twelve months. Many of those team members are still employees at Scheidler, some in supervisory capacities.

Once I had the players in place, the team began the process of re-engineering the entire information process. We observed, analyzed and documented every aspect of the company's operations. Using that information, we designed new streamlined processes aimed at providing timely, accurate information. This process took about 19 months.

In my third year with the Company, I led the team that converted all operating functions to IncrediblyHiTech software. I believe that is the platform that your company now uses.

Subsequently, I formed a team to develop a new cost accounting system. In 14 months, the team was able to improve the accuracy of the cost data substantially. The direct benefit of the new system was a reduction of inventory by over $10 million. Further, more accurate data generated by that system allowed Sales and Marketing to generate much more aggressive bids on high value sales opportunities.

In 2004, I was promoted to CFO. My new charter was to address the treasury function and to improve the balance sheet of the company. Working with the CEO, Tom Mason, we were able to recapitalize the company's debt, reducing our cost of capital dramatically. We also arranged for an infusion of private equity without a substantial dilution of current shareholder interests. The lower cost debt and new equity allowed us to acquire several key companies that contributed to our growth.

Scheidler International, as you may know, has been one of the strongest players in its field. Our balance sheet remains very strong, even with the setback that the industry is experiencing. I have enjoyed and still enjoy the business environment at Scheidler.

The opportunity that CressCorp has presented, though, has caught my attention. If my understanding is correct, the combination of my experience with your resources could be a win-win situation.

Allow me to stop here. I would be happy to discuss any part of my background in more detail."

Analysis of Mike's presentation:

- Mike's narrative adequately covered each employment situation listed on his resume. He furnished the size and a general description of each of his previous employers, listing his key responsibilities and accomplishments, as well as his reasons for leaving.
- He provided general information at the 20,000-foot level about his youth, education and early career.
- His descriptions became more detailed as his experience became more applicable to the current opportunity.
- He focused his presentation on his personal leadership, contributions and accomplishments, not the accomplishments of a group.
- He provided enough information to entice the interviewer, but not so much as to cause the dreaded glazing over of eyes.

If Mike's career summary has impressed the interviewer, the conversation should take on a life of its own at this point. His presentation should have inspired questions or a desire for further information.

If Mike's prospective employer is a manufacturer with sales between $300 million and $1 billion, international operations, unsatisfactory accounting functions, an outdated IT platform and/or an interest in lean methodology or team building, the company should be very interested in talking further with him.

On the other hand, if the company is a privately held company looking for a CFO to maintain the status quo, Mike's presentation has highlighted the wrong strength set, and may justifiably leave the interviewer believing him to be overqualified for the current opportunity.

---THE NON-CHRONOLOGICAL
RESUME REVIEW INTERVIEW---

To this point, we have discussed a chronological resume review format. The presentation progressed from the beginning of the candidate's career to the end, highlighting the most relevant experience segments. Most employers and candidates are very comfortable with this scenario because it allows them to follow a known time line and gives a semblance of organization to the interview.

However, keeping in mind that each interviewer is unique and not all interviewers are methodological or well-trained, you might be confronted with an interviewer who jumps from 2003 to 1995 to 2008 with nary a pause. My advice is to always have your resume at your fingertips so that you do not stumble over dates, mix up employers, or become extremely disoriented over the course of the interview.

Um, I'd like to plead the fifth about 2004

---SUMMARY---

The resume review interview format is one in which questions are derived directly from information contained in your resume. The format may consist of a series of direct, specific questions requiring concise, direct answers. Alternatively, an interviewer might begin with a more open-ended question, such as *"Tell me about your career up to this point,"* demanding a narrative style answer, followed by more detailed questions that target specific aspects of your background.

Here is a little headhunter advice to enhance your odds of success in a resume review interview:

- The tension of an interview can contribute to memory loss. Before any interview, study your resume to refresh your memory, especially regarding dates and long-ago positions.
- Keep your resume in front of you during the interview, so that you are able to refer to it when necessary.
- Verbally highlight your education and professional certifications, especially if you have top tier institutions in your pocket.

- Be prepared to expand upon the story told in your resume using examples and anecdotes to demonstrate your achievements. Achievements are the best selling tools.
- In your presentation, emphasize the portions of your career that most closely mirror the opportunity sought.
- Your focus should be on solving the needs of the interviewer using examples of prior experience.

INTERVIEW MASTER

Interviewer:

From your detailed description, it is clear that your experience as a financial analyst at Jack B. Nimble included many of the same responsibilities you would be facing as a senior financial analyst at our company. We see that as a major plus.

Chapter 9

Interview Formats:
The Behavioral Interview

Interviewer:
Tell me about a project you were involved in that did not go well and explain what you learned from that situation.

Candidate:
Hmmmm… there are so many…where do I begin?

The previous chapter examined the resume review interview format. The resume review interview consists of questions and answers derived directly from the items listed on a candidate's resume. Questions in a resume review interview are designed to fill in the resume outline with some additional factual details about a candidate's background.

As your career moves up the food chain, the positions you seek may be more demanding; the expectations of you as an individual contributor higher. The requirements of a middle to upper level position might include such traits as acute industry knowledge, superior technical expertise, proficiency at problem-solving, leadership ability, excellent communication skills, and team-building capabilities.

Evidence of these characteristics may be difficult to pinpoint on a resume; buried within a single line of a single paragraph or concealed behind a bulleted point. Uncovering these traits may require skilled digging and prying beneath the surface of the resume by an experienced interviewer. To expose these more nebulous attributes, a resume review interview might not suffice. Instead, your interviewer may select a behavioral interview format to elicit the information he wants.

If this is the case, get ready for the digging and prying.

---THE BEHAVIORAL INTERVIEW FORMAT---

Behavioral interviewing is based on a widely accepted proposition that the best predictor of future behavior is past performance. A behavioral interview is structured to analyze <u>in depth</u> how a candidate has performed in <u>specific</u> past instances as a means of determining how that candidate might act when presented with a comparable set of circumstances.

As an example, if the Governor of a state has raised taxes four times in succession when the budget analysis reflected a shortfall, it is likely that he or she will propose a tax increase the next time there is a budget problem (something to remember during the next election cycle). When a company is recruiting middle to upper management talent, the same connect-the-dots approach is utilized to judge a candidate.

Connecting the dots…not child's play

Because asking predictive questions and interpreting responses require some training and a large amount of insight, behavioral interviews are often conducted by experienced external recruiters, sophisticated human resource professionals, upper management, board members, investors, and/or the business owner(s); in other words, important people and/or people who think they are important.

Interview questions are formulated in advance of the interview based upon a side-by-side review of the candidate's resume and the requirements of the position. Questions are strategically designed to delve deeply into one or more situations a candidate has encountered, examining his actions, his thought processes, his level or involvement and his level of authority. Through this process, the interviewer hopes to measure specific strengths or weaknesses in the candidate based upon his past behavior.

Whereas I have described the resume review format as a "fill-in-the-blanks" format, I would call the behavioral format a "search-and-discover" mission, with each seemingly miniscule event in your career a potential hiding-place of information. Are you having fun yet?

> *As you might imagine, the behavioral interview can be much more challenging and unpredictable than the resume review interview. It may be nearly impossible for you to anticipate the direction the interview might take. Still, you can prepare for the interview by examining your resume with care and mentally reviewing your actions relating to specific events. If you have been given a written position description for the current opportunity, consider how elements on your resume might be applicable to the requirements listed in the position description.*

Do not panic when you encounter a behavioral interview. If you have prepared well for your interview; if your past actions demonstrate the experience, the industry exposure, and the skill set required to perform well in a job; your behavioral interview will give you an opportunity to display your excellence.

Behavioral Interview Example: Carolyn the Controller

In case you still feel understandably in the dark regarding what to expect at a behavioral interview, I'd like to shed some light over the murkiness. Using a sample resume from Chapter 3 as a foundation, I am going to walk through a behavioral interview scenario for fictional candidate Carolyn Johnson.

In this scenario, Carolyn is interviewing with the VP of Human Resources (Mr. Veep) at WinCo, a manufacturer that is seeking a Controller. (We will refer to only the most recent portion of Carolyn Johnson's resume for our example.)

RESUME OF:
CAROLYN JOHNSON
(Insert contact information here)

EDUCATION:

2002   **University of Chicago Graduate School of Business,** Chicago, Illinois
Masters of Business Administration -- Accounting

1994   **Indiana University Kelley School of Business,** Bloomington, Indiana
Bachelor of Science -- Accounting

CERTIFICATIONS:

· Certified Public Accountant (CPA) – Passed all four parts on first attempt
· Certified in Production and Inventory Management (CPIM) – Passed all six parts on first attempt

EXPERIENCE:

Jan 2005   **WONDERFUL WIDGETS, INC,** Wheaton, Illinois
To Present
              Controller

Manage the accounting and information technology departments for an $80 million division of a $400 million publicly traded manufacturing corporation. Participate as a key member of the corporate senior management team.

Responsibilities include:
· Develop corporate strategy in conjunction with other members of corporate senior management team.
· Oversee internal and external audit processes on a quarterly and annual basis (including Sarbanes Oxley).
· Assist in preparing the annual 10K and quarterly 10-Q.
· Create and maintain internal controls throughout the company.
· Direct integration of recent acquisitions and product line transfers.
· Prepare annual budgets and conduct financial analyses for senior management.
· Conduct internal audits at various international locations and support president of the international division.
· Assist with managing the overall operations of the division (production, supply chain management, HR).

Accomplishments:
· Developed a pricing model that allowed salesmen to structure large transactions with maximum flexibility for the customer while maintaining acceptable profit margins.
· Led the team that upgraded the IT system from Antique Systems to Most Impressive.

Jan 2001 to   **INGOODCOMPANY, INC.,** Indianapolis, Indiana
Dec2004
               Assistant Controller

Managed the accounting group for a $200 million privately held manufacturing company. Responsibilities included managing monthly accounting cycle and presenting analysis of financial statements to CFO and President.

Accomplishments:
· Created a comprehensive set of performance metrics to manage and track progress against corporate strategy.
· Provided president with blueprint for corporate restructuring, resulting in over $1 million cost reduction.
· Led the design and implementation of company-wide activity-based costing system, yielding better insight to primary cost drivers and profit margin by product.

March 1997   **BIG 4 PUBLIC ACCOUNTING,** Chicago, Illinois
To Jan 2001

etc.etc.etc. (edited for space reasons)

Prior to their meeting, Mr. Veep has reviewed Carolyn's resume and prepared questions for the interview. The goal of Mr. Veep's questions is to evaluate Carolyn's potential performance at WinCo. Unbeknownst to Carolyn, WinCo is considering a huge restructuring of the company in an order to reduce its costs.

Mr. Veep begins the interview by providing a description of WinCo and key information about the open position. Next, he turns to Carolyn's credentials.

Starting at the beginning of her resume, and moving forward chronologically, Mr. Veep spends about 20 minutes asking some general questions about Carolyn's education and her previous positions, seeking to fill in some blanks as to why Carolyn accepted each position, the work environment at the various companies, her responsibilities and major contributions, and her reasons for leaving each company. So far Carolyn has experienced a typical resume review interview.

But here begins the behavioral portion of the interview.

Because of WinCo's potential restructuring plans, Mr. Veep has taken a keen interest in Carolyn's "blueprint for corporate restructuring" project at InGoodCompany, Inc. (second bullet point). For the next hour, he focuses on uncovering every detail of this project and determining the extent of Carolyn's role in it. He asks about the scope of the project, what departments were involved, whether it was an individual or a team project, who made the decisions, what the budget was, how successful the results were, setbacks that occurred, return on investment, and most important, Carolyn's specific function.

Here is a summation of Carolyn's individual responses to Mr. Veep's questions regarding the corporate restructuring project.

"The president approached me to develop a restructuring plan taking into consideration the current market conditions and the company's perceived market advantages. He was concerned that the company's resources were not being matched with the brightest opportunities.

My first action was to set a plan that met the two month timeframe for delivery of the project. I then identified key operations personnel who would be able to provide valuable input and recruited nine people to this task force. Once the committee was complete, I led the process of outlining our mission statement. When questions arose during the project, we used this mission statement to clarify the appropriate path. Issues that became judgment call matters were ultimately decided by me.

My department provided historical financial data and analysis to each of the team members. Using historical data, team members developed actionable, detailed plans for their respective departments. As these individual plans were developed, I oversaw the work of each team member to assure that they were working in the correct space and keeping a good pace. I also contributed input to individual plans because of my knowledge of the overall project.

Once all the individual plans were complete, I arranged for my staff members to consolidate the information and return the preliminary results back to the group members. I then scheduled meetings for group members to discuss the plan in detail and in total.

Once the group was satisfied with the outcome, I summarized the data and prepared an overview document explaining the process, the people who were engaged, the findings and our suggestions. I delivered the final product to the president two weeks before the agreed deadline."

Analysis of Carolyn's behavioral interview:

- Note that Mr. Veep locked on to a single line in Carolyn's resume that was most relevant to WinCo's restructuring plans. A large portion of Carolyn's interview time was spent digging into this single item. The remainder of the resume was covered at the 20,000 foot level.
- Carolyn was obviously well-prepared to discuss the inner workings of the corporate restructuring plan and her role in it. Since she had no idea that Mr. Veep would focus all of his attention on that specific area of her background, it can be assumed that she was equally well-prepared to present other areas of her resume in comparable detail.

- Note the frequent use of the word "I" in Carolyn's response. Carolyn left no doubt as to who was in charge of the project. By using "I" instead of "we," Carolyn demonstrated ownership of the success of the project.
- Carolyn provided a generous amount of information about the project, including the exact nature of her responsibilities, the number of people involved, the time frame, and the step-by-step progress from initiation to culmination.
- While she nicely outlined the scope, people and responsibilities, Carolyn neglected to lay out the results of her work. What was the final outcome? How much of the final product was actually implemented; a portion or the entirety? How much money was saved as a result of the project? How did the new streamlined focus enable the company to compete more effectively?

The previous example illustrates the unpredictable path of a behavioral interview. Since you don't know what format your interview will follow until you are knee-deep into it, it is best to be well prepared for behavior-based questions by equipping yourself with many details and examples from your background.

Examples of Behavior-Based Questions

In case you are still a little foggy about what you might encounter in a behavioral interview, here are some additional examples of behavior-based questions.

- *"Please provide an example of how you have motivated a struggling staff member in the past."*
- *"Please give an example of a time when you were able to resolve a conflict with a less than cooperative co-worker?"*
- *"Can you provide some detail as to how you built your department at Zing Company? How did you motivate the staff on a weekly basis?"*

- *"What steps did you take to develop a market for the new NQ1 computer?"*
- *"Please tell me how you and your team developed this unique fluid pump? Be as specific as possible."*
- *"How did you go about acquiring seven companies in six months? What resources did you and your department require?"*
- *"Tell me in detail about a project that did not go well, and what you learned from that experience that you use today."*
- *"What has been your most humbling experience? Why and how does that influence you today?"*
- *"I see that last year you exceeded your sales quota by 100%. How did you do that?"*
- *"Give me an example of a time when you had to juggle your work priorities in order to meet deadlines."*

Note that behavioral questions tend to be open-ended, allowing the candidate great latitude in forming a response. Always keep in mind that the questions have been designed to determine a level of competency in a specific area such as leadership, team-building, management, technology, communication skills, or problem-solving. Try to determine what the interviewer is seeking in your answer.

---ANSWERING BEHAVIOR-BASED QUESTIONS---

The STAR method:

A veteran human resource professional and acquaintance notes that he uses the STAR method when he conducts a behavioral interview. STAR stands for Situation, Task, Action and Results. Every question this interviewer asks is focused on achieving the following:

- Recognizing what <u>Situation</u> on a resume might be relevant to his screening process;
- Discerning the <u>Task</u> that the candidate performed in this situation;

- Unearthing the <u>Action</u> a candidate took to complete that task; and
- Analyzing the <u>Results</u> or outcome of the situation.

Similarly, you as a candidate can use the STAR components to guide your answers to behavioral questions.

How did our fictional candidate Carolyn Johnson fare based on a STAR analysis of her answer? It appears that she did pretty well. She presented the situation (president's concern regarding utilization of the company's resources); the task (develop a restructuring plan); the action (recruit personnel, create a mission statement, supply and analyze information, schedule meetings, oversee staff, coordinate results, create the final presentation); and the result (the final plan delivered two weeks before deadline). Her presentation could have been even more effective had she provided even more information on the outcome of the project.

Use the "I" word

In a behavioral interview, it is mandatory that you speak in the first person and identify your accomplishments as an individual, avoiding use of the "we" word, which dilutes or mischaracterizes your achievements. "I" connotes leadership and accountability and management. "We" connotes a flock of sheep. Whenever possible, choose to begin sentences with *"I decided"* or *"I recruited"* or *"I wrote."* The behavioral interview is no place for modesty. Of course, what you say must be true.

Consider the following exchange during a behavioral interview:

Candidate: *"We developed a process that eliminated two very expensive operations previously required in the manufacture of milk chocolate."*

Interviewer: *"'We' is not being considered for a new job, you are. Did you have the initial idea? Did you manage the implementation process? Did you recruit the necessary players? What exactly was your role?"*

Some veteran recruiters believe that "we" candidates often seek to puff up their responsibilities, thereby grabbing some unearned gold. The gold will turn to dust when follow-up questions reveal that the puffing candidate was part of a team of 27 and played only a minor role in the outcome.

The two-minute answer rule

Behavior-based questions are generally open-ended. A candidate who loves the sound of his or her voice can be tempted to wander off the path or stray into the weeds. I suggest that when you answer questions, you remember the Beatles. Most early Beatles songs lasted roughly two-and-a-half minutes. The songs were upbeat and interesting and left you wanting more. Keep your answers to approximately two minutes, so that the interviewer is fully engaged throughout your presentation and is left wanting more information when you have finished. There are exceptions to this rule, for instance when an interviewer asks for a "walk-through" of your entire career or your life. If you can "walk-through" your career in two minutes, you had better be entry level.

Think before speaking

When you receive a behavior-based question, it is not expected that you will begin speaking immediately. You will not look bad if you take five or six seconds to analyze what your interviewer is looking for and compose your answer. Do not wait two-and-a-half minutes to begin your answer. But do not sacrifice content for speed.

---HYPOTHETICAL QUESTIONS---

As defined earlier, behavioral interviewing is based on the proposition that the best predictor of future behavior is past performance. Behavior-based questions are designed to elicit in-depth information about how a candidate performed in the past.

A variation on a behavior-based question is the hypothetical question, which attempts to predict future behavior by proposing an imaginary future situation and asking for the candidate's reaction. Here are some hypothetical questions:

- *"What would you do if you were walking through another department at your company and saw an employee viewing pornography on his computer?"*
- *"How would you mediate a conflict between two necessary members of your staff? Termination is not an option."*
- *"How would you deal with a situation in which a client lied about you to your boss?"*
- *What would you do if you found that the east coast was about to be overrun by locusts?*

Most professional interviewers do not find hypothetical questions useful because the candidate is not encumbered by current or historical facts. Nevertheless, hypothetical questions will arise, especially when an interviewer has been unsuccessful at drawing out the information he or she is seeking.

When asked a hypothetical question, your best and most valid response is to refer back to an actual, real-life experience that parallels the hypothetical situation and explain how you responded at that time.

A second option would be to answer the question based on a general business or ethical philosophy you espouse.

Or you can guess what the interviewer might like to hear. In a hypothetical, you are not constrained by reality.

---SUMMARY---

A behavioral interview is structured to dig deeply into one or more specific elements of a candidate's past performance to discover areas of competency that are deemed necessary to the role he or she is seeking. These areas of competency include but are not limited to industry knowledge, leadership, team-building, technical expertise, management, communication skills, or problem-solving. Behavioral questions tend to be open-ended, challenging, and may be hard to predict.

Behavioral interviews are common when interviewing for middle level and upper level positions, and behavior-based questions are becoming more widely used even at the lower levels of a career. To prepare for a behavioral interview, review your resume and refresh your memory regarding every position you have held and every accomplishment you list. If you prepare well, the behavioral format offers you a chance to market your candidacy in the best possible light, allowing you time to present your experience and your accomplishments in some detail.

INTERVIEW MASTER

Interviewer:

Tell me about a situation in which you had to deal with an unexpected setback and how you managed it.

Candidate:

One month after I was hired as a marketing associate for TweedleDee & TweedleDum Law Firm, the business development manager, whom I reported to, had a serious heart attack and was forced to take a lengthy medical leave. With very little training, I was required to take a leadership role planning a major corporate function that took place during her absence. Here's what I did...

Chapter 10

Interview Formats: A Random Walk

Interviewer:

Let me explain how today's interview will go...I will talk non-stop from beginning to end leaving you no time to inject a full sentence, then I will complain afterward that you did not provide enough information about yourself.

In the previous two chapters, I presented common, identifiable interview formats known as the resume review format and the behavioral format. In this chapter, I will attempt to describe an interview process which I will call the random walk, also known as the "just wing it" format or the "no-format" format. The random walk encompasses all interviews that do not proceed according to any distinguishable plan because...there is no distinguishable plan.

When I first entered the search business 25 years ago, my learning curve was steep. My on-the-job education involved recruiting techniques such as sourcing candidates and reading resumes critically. Other challenges included attracting clients to use my services. But when I look back at my early headhunter years, I realize that one of my biggest learning experiences came from listening to my candidates' interview feedback.

> ***Back in those days, I assumed that when I sent a candidate to a job interview, I could trust that he or she would be interviewed by a business professional prepared with the necessary skills to conduct an organized, methodical interview. Back in those days, I was wrong. Fortunately, my candidates quickly relieved me of my misconception.***

Some candidates would report back that their interview had been, at best, confusing; at worst, chaotic. Others described a friendly chat that never evolved to dealing with the opportunity at hand. A few described a monologue in which the interviewer talked for fifty minutes of an hour-long meeting. Still others reported a single-question scenario, in which the interviewer started and ended his presentation with one question: *"Why are you here?"* Several of my candidates were so taken aback that they were unable to quickly switch gears and develop a strategy for these unexpected interview formats. I was taken aback because I had prepared my candidates for interview formats that didn't occur.

If I had written this book for hiring managers, I would now address the methods in which a hiring manager should prepare and organize an interview. (Suffice it to say that there is a reason I make it my practice to actually be present in client/candidate interviews.) But since this is a book for candidates, I want to address what you, as a candidate, can do to make the best out of a non-traditional, unorthodox, random walk interview.

---THE RANDOM WALK---

Once most job interviews start, a recognizable format such as the resume review or behavioral format soon becomes obvious to a prepared candidate. This may give the candidate confidence as he or she has anticipated likely questions and planned a presentation accordingly. In such a case, dialogue begins to flow back and forth, and the interview proceeds to a successful outcome in which each party has provided and acquired a wealth of information.

However….while a well-planned interview with a pre-determined strategy is the ideal situation, occasionally the real diverges from the ideal. An unplanned or poorly executed interview may occur for a variety of reasons:

- Sometimes, an unprepared individual is thrust into a recruiting or hiring situation late in the process because the first-string player is absent or unavailable. This pinch hitter may lack familiarity with the nature and requirements of the position, so may revert to other more comfortable topics such as the candidate's personal life or the state of local sports.
- Unorthodox interviews are common in smaller, growing companies that lack experienced human resource professionals. Early stage entrepreneurial enterprises are likely culprits. You may be meeting with the business owner who is juggling five significant priorities. Your interview is number six.
- Alternatively, in a larger organization, you may find yourself meeting with a very accomplished professional such as a VP of engineering or a high-level finance or IT expert. These individuals tend to be very good at something; that something may not be conducting an interview.
- The personality of the interviewer definitely plays a large part in how an interview transpires. Occasionally, an interviewer loves the sound of his or her own voice and forgets to take a breath to allow the candidate into the conversation. Conversely, a shy or inexperienced interviewer may have planned few questions, relying on the candidate to carry the ball. Both of these situations can evolve into a one-sided monologue with lots of useless information divulged.

Whatever the underlying cause, some interviews simply don't follow a predictable pattern. These are the interviews I want to discuss in this chapter. These scenarios are a true test of your preparedness, your ability to adapt, and your people skills. With some forethought, even an unorthodox interview can become another opportunity to effectively sell your skills. Although there are an infinite number of random walk interviews, I am going to describe a few which I have been made aware of on more than one occasion.

---THE "TELL ME ABOUT YOURSELF" INTERVIEW---

A scenario that can make candidates quake is one in which the interviewer early and without warning delivers the ultimate open-ended question. After a friendly greeting and exchange of pleasantries, the interviewer leans back comfortably in her chair, smiles (or smirks), and issues the request (or command), *"Tell me about yourself."*

If you read Chapter 8 describing the resume review interview format, you will recognize similarities between this question and *"Walk me through your resume."* But whereas the resume walk-through request is at least somewhat confined to the elements you have chosen to list on your resume, *"Tell me about yourself"* provides virtually no direction to guide the candidate's answer.

A candidate who has not visualized this scenario may panic. *"Where do I start? Should I start with where I grew up...where I went to college? Does she want to know about my first part-time job 20 years ago? Do I mention that I am married/divorced/a mother of two?"* The extremely open-ended question can be overwhelming; the options for answering it innumerable.

A lazy or inexperienced interviewer might be likely to utilize the open-ended *"Tell me about yourself"* technique when detailed interview questions have not been prepared. On the other hand, the question might be part of a deliberate strategy employed by an expert, professional interviewer to evaluate a candidate's poise and communication skills, while getting a "feel" for the candidate as a person.

But if you are prepared for a question like this, the interviewer has just offered you a gift by ceding control of the interview session to you.

You now get to determine how to best highlight your strengths and avoid prolonged discussion of your limitations.

So what do you do? You pause, take a breath, and start talking. While I have previously recommended confining most of your answers to about two minutes, you should plan on an eight to ten minute presentation to answer an extremely open-ended, broad topic question.

Let's prepare for this presentation.

I suggest that your first step be to request permission to ask a few questions that will help you refine your response. *"To help me focus on what is important to you, may I ask a few questions before I begin?"* This request is almost always granted.

Two or three relevant questions at this time can help you narrow your response to *"Tell me about yourself"* from the very general to the specific. You might want to ask what specific skills are important in this position. You can ask if there are any specific positions on your resume that are of particular interest to your interviewer. Your interviewer's answers might touch on such issues as job content, supervisory responsibilities, IT platform, or strategy initiatives; all of which can help you construct a narrative that is centered upon your interviewer's needs. For example, the interviewer's response to one of your questions may lead you to emphasize times in your career when you have implemented staff changes.

A secondary benefit of asking a few targeted questions is gaining some time to organize your thoughts into a cohesive presentation. Of course you do not want to appear to be evading the interviewer's request for information. After a few brief questions to help you outline what you want to say, you need to say it. Having absorbed the input from the employer's answers, you are ready to begin your presentation, weaving a story that incorporates and emphasizes your relevant experience.

I recommend that you start your response at the 20,000-foot level regarding your early life, providing a few "prime" morsels of information from your childhood/adolescence that may have helped shape you as a person. Here are some ideas:

⇒ Were you an only child; one of six siblings?

⇒ Did you move frequently throughout your childhood?

⇒ Did you live abroad for an extended period?

⇒ Did you follow in one of your parents' career footsteps?

⇒ Did you have a job at a young age?

⇒ Were you a varsity athlete in high school; star of high school musicals; member of the national champion debate team (an interview should be a walk in the park)?

⇒ Did you get a college scholarship; work your way through college?

⇒ How did you decide what college to attend; what major to pursue?

More than a few minutes dealing with your childhood and early education is too much. Any mention of partying, popularity, or prom is much too much.

Continue the fly-over pattern until your experience begins to relate significantly to the position at hand. (If you are an entry level candidate, this may be your college classes and internships.) At this point, your presentation should begin to resemble an open-ended resume review narrative.

As your positions and responsibilities begin to closely resemble the company's current needs, zero in for a landing, complete with detailed descriptions and relevant examples drawn from specific instances in your career. Do not hesitate to present experience that is close, but not a perfect match.

Refer to your resume if necessary to keep from venturing off track. You may or may not get all the way through your presentation. A single experience that you highlight in the first few minutes may be the basis for an interruption that steers the remainder of the interview. Don't fight the fact that you are not being allowed to complete your full narrative. A win-win situation occurs when a previously unprepared interviewer is now actively engaged in the conversation.

If you sense that your presentation is not effective, it is acceptable and advisable to interrupt your own presentation with some follow-up questions to the interviewer. These questions might resemble the following:

- *"Based upon our discussion so far, do you feel my experience with planning corporate seminars is similar to what has been done here in the past?"*
- *"What are your thoughts to this point regarding my supervisory experience compared to your needs?"*
- *"How does my experience with PAS software correspond to what I would need in this position?"*
- *"Is the information I have provided to this point helpful to you?"*

The feedback you receive provides an opportunity to clarify details or re-direct your presentation. Removing yourself from a walk down the path to oblivion can literally keep your chances of success alive.

I recommend leaving personal details out of your narrative unless they are relevant to some aspect of your career. For example, you could include *"I relocated to Colorado after earning my MBA because my new wife had a great opportunity there and my credentials were very marketable in any location."* But there is no reason to share that you are in the process of dissolving your second marriage, dating a hockey player, or engaged in a tense custody battle.

To prepare for this type of question, visualize in advance of any interview how you might respond if such a question is posed. Once you have given some thought to your response, I recommend rehearsing your version of *"This is my life!"* at home before going live.

---THE "MONOPOLY" INTERVIEW---

Interviews in which one party monopolizes the time and the discussion are BAD NEWS. As a candidate, you should guard against talking for lengthy, uninterrupted stretches. One of my former partners once told a long-winded candidate *"If you see that the interviewer's eyes have rolled back in his head, you should assume that you have talked him to death."* A good interview is balanced. The interviewer is sharing information about the company and the role. The candidate is presenting his strengths and capabilities. No one has talked anyone to death.

In some cases, a boorish (or boring) interviewer may be the one doing the non-stop nattering. If this is the case, the candidate has little control, but may still end up the loser because the interviewer will not have gathered enough information to make a qualified decision. It is difficult to come up with a justification for hiring someone whose entire presentation ended with the initial *"Good morning."*

If you find yourself in an interview with a monopolizing interviewer, you have a couple of options. Blurting out *"Take a breath!!"* is not one of them, as satisfying as it might seem at the time. No matter how rude your interviewer is, a rude interruption on your part will immediately disqualify you from consideration.

Your best bet is to count on the need for air and be prepared to quickly inject your voice into the silent pause for inhaling. Listen for any word or sentence in the interviewer's presentation upon which you might build some groundwork for your candidacy. In order to get a figurative foot in the door, you may inject *"Oh yes. I have seen that exact situation at my former company,"* or *"I know what you mean. We use the same software platform at my company."* Your hope is that your interviewer will hear you, show some interest, and ask you for some detail. Once you have been acknowledged, you can begin to present your experience, highlighting your personal involvement.

If your interviewer is determined to talk through the session, there isn't a great deal you can do other than try to inject your input whenever possible. Recognizing that your time may be limited, it is critical that you express yourself concisely, focus like a laser on your ability to do the job, and provide clear cut examples.

Don't spend time worrying about your lack of input at this type of interview. Try to remember that an ill-mannered interviewer may be indicative of a job you don't want.

Now that you've read me the entire employee handbook, I'd like to interject a few words about my background...

---THE "WHEREVER IT LEADS" INTERVIEW---

For very senior positions such as CEO, CFO, Treasurer, COO, GM, or VP, it is not unusual for a candidate to meet with Board members as part of the selection process. It is my observation that interviews at this level are among the hardest to predict. Conversations may range from minutia regarding a patent to a candidate's philosophy regarding off-shoring.

I ***know of a circumstance*** *in which a candidate had survived several interviews with HR and various VPs and was a finalist for the position being offered. His last meeting was with the Chairman of the firm. In that meeting, no resume was referenced, no specific reference was made to prior company experience, nor was he asked about his greatest accomplishment. For nearly an hour, they discussed various business matters that had recently been covered in the Wall Street Journal.*

In preparing for such an interview scenario, I suggest that you learn everything possible about the individual you are meeting, in addition to conducting your normal interview research. His or her educational background, prior employment or investment activity, club memberships and/or charitable activities are all potential food for conversation. You never know when an insignificant item in your background will produce the spark for a lasting relationship.

*O*ne of my summer jobs *while in college was that of a night watchman in a greenhouse (hey, someone has to make sure the plants don't walk away!). It was a terribly boring, lonely job that cured me of ever wanting to work nights in isolation. Flash forward almost twenty years. I was now in the search business and calling on the owner of a rapidly growing, commercial greenhouse. Early in the conversation, I mentioned that I spent some time working in a greenhouse. The owner immediately had a dozen questions regarding my summer job. We became soul mates. Soon afterward, he awarded an assignment to my firm.*

My long-ago greenhouse experience did not win me the assignment, but it did allow for a cordial, comfortable meeting during which I was able to describe the resources and benefits of my firm. Knowing something about your interviewer's interests can provide the bridge from an examination of facts to a warmer evaluation of you as a total person.

Your listening skills are critical in senior level interviews. As your interviewer sets the agenda, you should be looking for any hint as to significant business drivers for this individual. Any answers offered should take these hints into consideration. Remember to hear and see your answers through the ears and eyes of the interviewer.

Never be intimidated by an interview with a high-level executive or Board member. Remember that this individual would not be asked to waste his or her time with a candidate who was not highly qualified for an executive level position. Treat this person as an equal, with the respect due an equal.

---SUMMARY---

Random walk interviews can be unnerving and frustrating to unsuspecting candidates and to the coaches who attempt to prepare the candidates for their interviews. These interviews follow no predictable pattern which can be taught to a candidate.

Nevertheless, if you have prepared for your interview with research on the company, the position, and the individual(s) involved, and have refreshed your memory on details of your background, you will be up to the challenge. As in every interview format, your primary goal is to identify the need of the company and communicate how you can be the solution.

My advice when preparing for a random walk is:

1. Review your research on the company and the interviewer.
2. Rehearse your presentation of experience. Prepare several scenarios ranging from short, question-and-answer type to a free flowing eight to ten minute talk about your life.
3. Don't hesitate to take control of the meeting if offered. You can then tailor your presentation to highlight your strengths and veer away from your limitations.
4. If you feel the meeting is not tracking well, ask questions that may provide an opportunity to re-direct your focus.
5. Understand that some interviews are destined to "crash and burn." If you were prepared for the interview and made your best effort to deliver your presentation, the failure was probably on the part of the interviewer. Assume it is the company's loss and move on without regrets.

$ $ $
INTERVIEW MASTER

Interviewer:

Tell me about yourself.

Candidate:

Before I begin, may I ask a question or two? Thank you!
(Questions asked.)
As I understand your need, this role will be best served by someone who has plastics industry experience and deep knowledge of the Midwestern market. Am I correct? Excellent, let me focus on my experience in those areas.

Chapter 11

Answering the Tough Questions:
Umm-m-m's the Word

INTERVIEW DISASTER

Interviewer:
Why were you laid off at RatCorp?

Candidate:
They falsely accused me of extorting $40,000 from the company.

Interviewer:
You're kidding. That's interesting. What really happened?

Candidate:
It was $30,000.

When I prepare a candidate for an upcoming interview, I usually close the conversation with the advice to *"Have fun!"*

I'm sure many of my candidates would like to slug me. After all, how much fun is it to have your past placed under a microscope, dissected, examined, and possibly rejected, all in the space of about two hours?

Point taken.

Yet I do think a job interview can be an experience to approach enthusiastically. When you arrive at your interview, you have already been selected as someone who might fit into this company's plans and aspirations. The people there are looking forward to meeting you. The attractive office in which you are nervously sweating may become your career home for several years. The individuals you see around you may be the ones with whom you will share coffee breaks and lunch hours and entertaining conversations about nothing. The position you are hoping to fill may enable you to pay for your children's college tuitions.

And if that's not exciting enough, think of it this way. How often do you get an hour or more to talk about the impressive things you have accomplished to someone who really cares? An interviewer may be the most interested listener you will encounter in months, spouse or significant other included. And most interviewers will go the extra mile to make your experience enjoyable, to ensure that you leave your interview with only positive things to say about the company.

Yet, as much fun as it is, before it is all over, chances are great that you will be asked a tough question or two that will provide a little break from the good times. My wife (and co-author and editor) reports responding to a question from the blind side during a job interview with a powerful and compelling seven-second *"Ummmm-m-m-m-m,"* before coming up with a passable answer. As wonderful and intelligent as she is, she did not earn the position. Over my years as a headhunter, I have heard many variations of that *"Ummmm-m-m-m-m,"* usually followed by the same result.

The purpose of this chapter is to expose you to some of the difficult interview questions I have heard and/or heard about during my career and to encourage you to begin preparing your answers to questions such as these. Of course, I cannot anticipate every curveball question that may be tossed out by a creative interviewer. But I can provide you with some examples of questions I've heard more than once and some suggestions as to how you might answer them. Even better, I can try to teach you a way of thinking that will prepare you to answer all the countless unanticipated interview questions you could encounter.

As you read this list of questions and responses, I recommend that you refer back to Chapter 6, which describes "thinking across the desk." If you manage to maintain a consistent focus on what your interviewer is seeking to discover through his or her questions, half the battle in the question-and-answer war is won.

> *Keep in mind that poise, confidence and sincerity can work wonders in masking imperfect responses.*

Consider rehearsing answers to potential questions at home in front of a mirror. As silly as you might feel, a brief rehearsal beforehand might save you from making a fatal error when it counts. Remember that each person's story is different and there is no single right or wrong answer to a question.

Correction. A lie or deception is always a wrong answer. The truth, when explained in an open and reasonable fashion, is always the better choice.

Here is a list of some tough questions I have either delivered or heard more than once in an interview setting:

1. <u>Briefly</u> explain, what do you do?

2. If you have had such great success at XYZ Co., why are you considering leaving your current job?

3. Why have you changed jobs so often?

4. Why were you laid off?

5. Why are you willing to accept this (lesser) position? Will you be sufficiently challenged here?

6. Describe a past situation in which.....

7. "What if..." or "If...what" questions

8. What do you like to do outside of work?

9. Where do you see yourself in five years?

10. What do you see as your greatest strength?

11. What would your last boss list as your top three strengths?

12. What do you see as your greatest weakness?

13. Have you hired anyone? If so, what attributes did you seek?

14. Have you fired anyone? Roughly, what were the circumstances that led to that action being taken?

15. Are you willing to relocate in two years?

16. Can you function with a remote boss?

17. How do you feel about reporting to three individuals?

18. What resources can we provide to help you grow in your career?

19. What is your current salary? What are your salary expectations?

20. How would you solve our problem?

21. So, are you interested in this position?

If you are feeling slightly uneasy by now, let's look at how you might answer some of these questions.

QUESTION 1: Briefly explain, what do you do?

Seems simple enough, doesn't it? Yet, when I was asked a similar question recently, I could only respond with stunned silence.

*W**hile having breakfast** with a colleague and discussing this book, the colleague, who happens to host a radio show part-time, posed a question he might ask me if I were trying to promote the book on his show. He wanted the answer in brief, sound bite form. "Why would someone buy your book?" For some unknown reason, I was struck* *dumb, emphasize the dumb. I did not even manage the seven-second "Ummm-m-m" response. I opened my mouth, then closed it, then opened it once again, waiting for my muse to inspire me. My muse had apparently been furloughed. I made a mental note to mention the scenario in the book. Here it is.*

Unlike this author, you should prepare a short answer, perhaps one to three paragraphs, that defines your principle responsibilities and duties and emphasizes your strengths. Here is an example.

"I am a marketing assistant for a well-known pharmaceuticals company. My responsibilities entail preparation of marketing literature, planning and coordinating major events such as nationwide seminars and trade shows, composing all correspondence related to these events, and often acting as the company's primary representative at the events. Although my title is 'assistant,' my supervisor travels 90% of the time, so I often perform the duties more typical of a 'coordinator' position."

QUESTION 2: If you have had such great success at XYZ Co., why are you considering leaving your current job?

There may be many truthful answers to a single question. Your answers during an interview should always display a positive and future-focused attitude on your part. In other words, when asked why you are leaving a position, you might want to avoid providing negative motives like hatred of your boss, fear of getting fired for cause, difficulty of job content, boredom, frustration with your workload, excessive overtime, discontent with your salary, or resentment of your co-workers. Even if one or more of the above conditions contributes to your desire for a new position, it is advisable to frame your answer in positive rather than negative terms.

Attempt to give an answer that revolves around your hopes for the future and how a job change can facilitate accomplishment of your career goals. Here are some examples:

- I have been with this company for two years and feel that my learning curve has flattened.
- I have become proficient in X area during my time at this company; now I would like to broaden my exposure within the Y area. That is not possible in my current company.
- While I enjoy working at MyCurrent Company, I do not see much opportunity for movement or growth within the company.
- I have enjoyed my work at MyCurrent Company, but I now feel that I would like to try a different course.
- During my time at MyCurrent Company, I received a little exposure to X area and it really stimulated my interest in that area.
- I have enjoyed working at Big Corporation, but I think Little Company might be a better fit for me.
- I have learned a lot about my strengths during my term at MyCurrent Company. I would like to find a position that really utilizes those strengths.
- I am very happy at MyCurrent Company, but I have been keeping my eyes open for attractive positions like this one.
- I enjoy working at MyCurrent Company, but this opportunity would expand my career possibilities substantially.
- My current job demands a high level of travel. Since my children came into the picture, I am facing increased family responsibilities and would like to limit my travel.

QUESTION 3: Why have you changed jobs so often?

If your resume lists a series of short-term jobs (less than two years duration in most professions), you will probably need to provide an explanation. Generally speaking, an employer does not want to envision training you and hiring your replacement before your two-year anniversary with the company. That said, there are many acceptable reasons for making job changes. During your interview, it is in your best interest to tell the truth, while using terms that are acceptable to your interviewer. Here are some acceptable answers related to job changes:

- My employer went out of business. (No further explanation needed.)
- The industry I was in was struggling financially. I could not be choosy and accepted some positions that were not ideal.
- I accepted a position that took my career in the wrong direction. When an opportunity came to correct my mistake, I took it.
- There was a misrepresentation of the position during the interview process.
- Leaving that company was a mistake. If I had the opportunity to do it over again, I would approach my manager and try to correct the situation before it reached the breaking point.
- I have always worked well with people, but the environment in that particular company was toxic due to changes in management.
- I had learned everything I could learn there and I was concerned that I was stagnating personally and professionally.
- There was no opportunity to move up within the company.
- I could see that the company was in bad financial shape. When a recruiter approached, I listened.
- I left when I was recruited into a position where both the salary and the responsibilities were at a much higher level.
- I made the choice to change career direction completely.

Almost any honest answer can be acceptable during an interview, when accompanied by a reasonable explanation. (Exception: Hard work or long hours should not be mentioned as reasons for job changes.) Try to reflect realistically and positively on your past, focus on what you have learned from each or your jobs, and speak freely about your hopes for the future. Shape your answers to your current interview. If the position for which you are interviewing provides no visible opportunity for growth, do not focus on a previous job's lack of upward mobility. If you are pursuing a people management position, do not dwell on past conflicts with your co-workers.

If your frequent job changes were in the distant past and your recent history reflects more stability, minimal explanation may be required. If your series of job changes is recent, you may have a bit of explaining to do.

QUESTION 4: Why were you laid off?

The previous question dealt primarily with job changes that were of your choosing. Along the way, you may have left a company involuntarily. The interviewer will have serious questions about why this occurred. How you respond will be of great consequence to the success or failure of your interview. Here are some realistic answers.

- The company went out of business.
- The company was in trouble. A fourth of the marketing department was eliminated.
- I got in over my head. The position was a little too advanced for my skill set at the time.
- The sales quotas were impossible to meet, given the economic times.
- There was some political in-fighting. When my boss was fired, I was fired with her.
- The department in which I worked was understaffed and poorly managed. None of us could perform well.
- I was not the right fit for that particular company environment.
- I should have stuck with what I'm good at rather than venturing into management.

As you might guess, each of these answers will open up additional lines of questioning. My advice is to stick to the truth, admit mistakes, and explain how you have learned and improved from your past experience.

During your interview, do not get bogged down with past mistakes or regrets about what has occurred in the past. Remember that you have

Answering the Tough Questions | 133

been selected based on the resume you provided. The faults in your background are already known. You are being given the chance to explain them. Do it with confidence and optimism about the future. **Be positive!**

Honesty is of the utmost importance here. The world truly is a small world. If you try to lie about a mistake in the past, there is a great possibility that your lie will be discovered; even if it is not discovered, you will live each day with the fear that it will.

QUESTION 5: Why are you willing to accept this (lesser) position? Will you be sufficiently challenged here?

If you are interviewing for a position with a lesser title than one you have previously held, the interviewer will be interested in your reasons. This is not a trick question; a prospective employer wants to get a sense for the level or responsibility that will keep you satisfied and happy.

Here some acceptable answers for this one:

- Although I did hold the (higher) title at XYZ Company, the scope of responsibilities was very similar to what is listed in your job description.
- While I was, in fact, previously a (higher title), the parts of the job that I most enjoyed are the ones I will be focusing on in this opportunity.
- Yes, I was previously a (higher title), but the economic climate is such that it may be hard to replicate that position. Based on your description of this position, I would find it very challenging and rewarding.
- I did not like certain aspects of the (higher) role. I am much more comfortable in this function.

QUESTION 6: Describe a past situation in which.....

Some of the most difficult questions you encounter will be the *"Describe a past situation"* questions, typical of a behavioral type interview. These will be the ultimate test of your memory, your communication skills and your poise under pressure.

Be prepared to draw on your experiences that have involved one or more of the following: conflict resolution; management styles; meeting tight deadlines; prioritization of tasks; delegating duties; technology problems; good or poor training; asking for or giving help; fair allocation of labor; time management; dealing with clients; dealing with the public; preparing or making presentations; etc.

I cannot, nor can you anticipate every *"Describe a situation"* question that might come up. I can simply advise you to be prepared to relate a number of detailed, true stories of experiences that might demonstrate your specific skills, strengths or qualifications for this job.

QUESTION 7: "What if..." or "If...what" questions

Politicians often refuse to answer hypothetical questions. You, on the other hand, have no choice but to answer the questions of the interviewer if you want to be considered for the position he or she controls. Be prepared for one or more *"If...what"* questions during your interview. Here are some examples:

- If you were asked to change an estimate to make the assumption more credible, even though you knew it was wrong, what would you do?
- If one of your reports routinely arrived to work 15 minutes late, what would you do?
- If you were given a completely unrealistic deadline for a project, what would you do?
- If your boss directed you to provide information that you knew was incorrect, what would you do?

Most of the *"If...what"* questions will relate to ethical issues, people management, or time management issues. No one can possibly predict the specific nature of each of these questions. Put simply, give some thought to workplace ethics, management style, and your relationships with co-workers before arriving at the interview.

QUESTION 8: What do you like to do outside of work?

As with the other questions, there is no one correct answer to this question. There are, however, some wrong answers, which include: sleeping, watching hours of TV, or enjoying a bottle of wine every night, among others.

You are a multi-faceted person with many interests. The interviewer does not want to know everything about you but would like to gain insight into you as an individual. Focus on describing the elements of your life that display physical activity, curiosity, social interaction, intellectual pursuits and an overall engagement with life and with the community. Focus on interests that complement the job opportunity.

QUESTION 9: Where do you see yourself in five years?

This question is often asked by an employer who is trying to get a grasp on whether this job and this company are the right fit for you. There are a number of correct answers. Not among these are *"I hope to be married and raising a baby at home,"* or *"I hope to be drinking margaritas in the Bahamas."*

Your answer should always reflect ambition and the desire to learn and grow within your field. Avoid answers that might indicate a desire for a radical shift in career direction.

Some appropriate answers might be:

- I would like to be at the regional management level in this firm.
- I would like to be one of your most successful salespeople.
- I would like to be qualified for a supervisory role within this department.
- In five years, I would like to have accomplished enough in this role to be eligible for the next level.

- I hope to perform in such a manner that I would be the first one considered for new growth opportunities.
- I would like to have had a substantial impact on your success so that upon your promotion, I may have your job.

QUESTION 10: What do you see as your greatest strength?

In our culture, we are taught from earliest childhood not to brag, so proudly proclaiming your strengths can sometimes cause vague discomfort. I suggest that you leave modesty behind, at least for the duration of your job interview. Be prepared to provide a short list of your strengths, as well as some concrete examples to back up these strengths. Workplace strengths might include: being a team player; technological proficiency; attention to detail; consistency; in-depth knowledge; accuracy; listening skills; leadership; sales skills; even temper; management skills. Think back on evaluations you have received from previous managers – what did they like about you? I suggest that you do not use "hard-working" or "honest" as your greatest strengths, as your interviewer will assume everyone he or she interviews will work hard and not steal the company's laptop.

QUESTION 11: What would your last boss list as your top three strengths?

This question is what I consider the equivalent of a free throw in basketball. As mentioned in the previous paragraph, it is very hard for most people to say *"I am great at this or that."* That dynamic changes when you have been given license to surmise what your boss would say. Be ready with three attractive and job related skills so that you can calmly and assuredly relate what your boss thinks your strengths are. This is a free opportunity to brag. Make good use of it.

Some examples:

- Grasps things quickly
- A leader among his/her peers
- Great attention to detail
- Easy to work with
- Analytical

- A positive force in the office
- Self-directed
- Intelligent
- Strong ability to multi-task
- A problem-solver

QUESTION 12: What do you see as your greatest weakness?

Ahh, the dreaded "weakness" question. There really is no perfect answer to this question, because a weakness is, after all, a weakness. Try mentally changing the word "weakness" to the phrase "area for improvement." It may make this question somewhat easier.

I recommend that you answer this question with a trait that is minor, that you are aware of, and that is correctible, and/or already corrected. Avoid mention of your personal life and problems; stick to workplace issues. For instance, *"In the past, I have had trouble delegating to my staff, but after I became aware of the problem, I really worked to become better at it."* Or *"Prioritizing my workload used to be a problem, so I got into the habit of making a list at the beginning of each day and referring to it periodically."*

QUESTION 13: Have you hired anyone? If so, what attributes did you seek?

Obviously, you will only be asked about hiring if you have previously been in a management role where hiring authority was a possibility. Be aware that this is a question an interviewer might use to find out indirectly about your management style, your work ethic, and your work priorities.

Attributes you might seek while hiring someone might include: track record of success; evidence of problem solving ability; ability to work independently; experience dealing with detailed reports; evidence of verbal and written communication skills; ability to work as a team. There is no one correct answer. Be prepared to give an answer that will reveal positive things about you. As you provide benchmarks, make sure you can pass your own test.

QUESTION 14: Have you fired anyone? Roughly, what were the circumstances that led to that action being taken?

This question is asked to determine your management style, the level of authority you have been given in the past, and your ability to cope with high-stress situations. The question can also reveal what things are important to you in the people with whom you will be working. Be prepared to answer what problems resulted in your firing someone and what remedial steps you took to deal with that situation before resorting to firing. The question may indicate that your new job will entail the firing of some current personnel.

QUESTION 15: Are you willing to relocate in two years?

If true, the correct answer is: *"Of course, I cannot predict the future, but given my current situation, I can definitely see myself being open to the possibility of relocation in a few years."*

If relocation will be required and you are not and never will be open to the possibility of moving, be honest with yourself and your potential employer. Even if you are currently unemployed, it is unethical and unwise to accept a position under false pretenses. Do not assume that you will find a way to avoid the relocation requirement. More probably, in two years you will be facing a furious employer and the prospect of seeking new employment with a very bad reference in your portfolio.

QUESTION 16: Can you function with a remote boss?

If you have never experienced a remote boss, you probably will not be able to answer this question definitively. A good, acceptable answer would be, *"Although I have never worked with a remote boss, I have always been able to work independently with reasonable direction. In the absence of a supervisor, I have learned to seek answers from many sources and to solve most problems on my own. And with current technology, it is often possible to make contact with a remote boss if necessary."*

QUESTION 17: How do you feel about reporting to three individuals?

Everyone knows that reporting to several managers, each with his or her own agenda, is a conflict waiting to happen. If the position for which you are interviewing requires reporting to more than one supervisor, the following would be an acceptable answer to the above question: *"I would enjoy the variety and the learning potential of working for several bosses. I can envision some problems with competing priorities among the three managers. If this began to happen, it would be my responsibility to approach my managers and inform them of the problem. I would not wait until deadlines were about to expire before notifying the managers that I had a workload problem."*

QUESTION 18: What resources can we provide to help you grow in your career?

A good answer would be, *"I would want the degree of personal and technological support necessary to enable me to perform well in this position. I am sure that you, as a successful company, will provide me with the tools I need to accomplish my job."*

QUESTION 19: What is your current salary? What are your salary expectations?

Among the trickiest questions to answer at job interviews are those relating to salary, past and potential. A would-be employer might, rightfully or wrongly, use your previous salary or your salary expectations to define your previous level of responsibility. For instance, an employer seeking to fill a position with a designated salary of $120,000 might look warily at the abilities of someone who is currently earning a salary of $85,000. An employer offering a salary that is less than what you currently earn might foresee potential discontent on your part.

In social situations, polite conduct prohibits any discussion of salaries and earnings. Even in a job interview, an interviewer may feel it is somewhat forward to directly ask a candidate his or her current or most recent salary. Many companies require the information on a written job application. Nevertheless, an employer just might broach the issue directly. If salary questions are raised during an interview, I recommend that you answer them forthrightly. Evasiveness or avoidance of the issue will likely be noticed and held against you.

Depending on how your interviewer frames the salary question, you may be able to word your answer in terms of salary expectations. When providing salary expectations, it is always best to use a somewhat wide range, such as upper $80s to mid $90s. Be generous with yourself when providing a salary range, as you will rarely get offered a salary exceeding that range. But not too generous; if the range that you provide is well above the available salary for the position, your interviewer may assume that you will not be satisfied with the company's offer.

If you want to work with an external recruiter, you must answer the salary question. My clients expect that information from me and will not pursue a candidate who refuses to provide it. In the normal course of evaluating candidates, I ask about current compensation in both specific numbers and components. There is no point trying to put a size 14 CFO into a size 10 CFO role or vice versa. On rare occasions, a candidate will refuse to share salary information with me. That is his or her privilege. But it is my standard practice to part company with that candidate in short order.

If you really prefer not to discuss salary information, you can respond to related questions with a statement such as, *"I assume that any offer you would make would be reasonable for a position of this level."* You must live with the consequences of your insistence on privacy.

QUESTION 20: How would you solve our problem?

Very few people from outside an organization can meaningfully generate answers to an entity's ongoing challenges. Assume that this question is designed to begin a conversation that will provide insight into your style and problem-solving abilities. Don't worry about details. Ask questions to establish a base of assumption. Deal with steps you would take in identifying the situation and several potential actions you would suggest.

Most importantly, at this stage, you are not responsible for providing a single correct answer. You are responsible for demonstrating your ability to solve problems.

QUESTION 21: So, are you interested in this position?

Even if your interviewer is Ebenezer Scrooge, the corporate office is roach-infested, and the position takes you down three rungs on the career ladder, it is safest to answer this question in the affirmative, at least after an initial interview. After expending the time and effort to prepare for and participate in an interview, there is no point in terminating the process prematurely. Answer yes, then go home and take a few hours or an overnight to consider whether the position is worth pursuing. If you elect not to go forward, you can simply inform the company of your change of heart the next day. Do not accept a second interview if there is less than 50% chance that you will accept the position.

If this question is asked at a second or third interview, you can qualify your positive response with one or two special considerations you might have. Always keep in mind that an unenthusiastic candidate will probably not be hired.

---SUMMARY---

It is impossible to anticipate each and every question that you might encounter during your job interview. Every job has different requirements and every interview evolves differently. But I encourage you to examine the thinking process used to formulate the above responses and try to apply that thinking process to the unique questions you receive. Prepare examples and short narratives that can be used to support your various strengths. Be prepared to discuss and support the choices you have made that have brought you to where you are today. Practice your answers. And focus on the following goals as you answer each question:

- Try to discern what information the interviewer is trying to glean from the question;
- Make an effort to provide that information in a calm, straightforward fashion;
- Focus on the positive rather than the negative in any given situation;
- Formulate answers that are straightforward and truthful, and emphasize your strengths;
- Confine most answers to approximately two minutes.
- Be positive, be positive, be positive!

INTERVIEW MASTER

Interviewer:
What do you enjoy doing outside of work?

Candidate:
I love to test myself both physically and mentally. I am currently preparing to compete in September's Triathlon with several of my friends. I am also taking two graduate level business classes at the U of Z, so I don't have a lot of free time.

Chapter 12

Special Interview Challenges:
Food for Thought

INTERVIEW DISASTER

Interviewer:
I'm sorry, but that big glob of red sauce on your chin is distracting me.
Here's a napkin.

By now, you have learned that each interview is a unique composition of elements which can culminate in either a successful showcasing of your talents or a failure to connect. While all interviews present challenges, it has been my experience that when those challenges include table manners, marinara sauce, or fall-off-the-bone ribs, the opportunities for "the big mistake" multiply dramatically. In this chapter, I'll address survival in restaurant interview settings and other common challenging interview situations. Topics include the following:

— Interviewing over food;
— The team interview;
— Marathon interviewing;
— The interview by subordinates.

---INTERVIEWING OVER FOOD: YOU VS. RIBS---

Most job interviews are conducted in an office setting during business hours. But there are many circumstances, such as those that follow, in which an office interview is not possible or preferable:

- My goal as a recruiter is to make it as painless as possible for a prospective candidate to join the interview process. With that objective, I often travel to a location near to the candidate's place of employment, and schedule time and venue based on the candidate's availability, usually before or after working hours.
- On many occasions, I have recruited candidates from geographic locations requiring air travel (mine or theirs). To expedite the interview schedule, I often arrange meetings at a public location convenient to the airport or the candidate.
- Confidentiality concerns and/or work flow disruptions may influence a company to avoid on-site interviews, instead selecting the option of meeting away from the office or plant.
- The desire to observe a candidate in a relaxed setting, rather than across a desk or conference table, may cause an employer to choose an off-site interview.

When an off-site interview is selected, it becomes necessary to find a comfortable, accessible place where conversation can flow freely. More often than not, that location is a restaurant or coffee shop. With this in mind, I think it might be helpful to provide some advice on interviewing while eating.

Tips for Restaurant Interviews

1. IN ADVANCE, DETERMINE HOW TO MEET AND IDENTIFY YOUR INTERVIEWER.

*I*t *may not be necessary* to wear a red rose in your lapel, but providing a general description of yourself including height, hair color, or what you will be wearing will help to facilitate an early introduction and prevent awkward overtures to strangers.

Recently, a referred candidate and I wasted valuable time because we had not thought to designate in advance how we would identify one another. I sat drinking coffee at a table while my candidate stood waiting in the lobby, each assuming the other would make his presence known. I, of all people, should know better.

I typically arrive at a restaurant before my candidate makes an appearance. I will advise the restaurant host I would like to be seated and provide my name. Additionally, I ask the host if he will keep an eye open for the person I am meeting and show him/her to the table.

If you as the candidate arrive before the interviewer, you can similarly ask to be seated and have the host direct the interviewer to the table. I find it more comfortable to sit at a table than in the lobby of a restaurant.

2. EAT, DRINK, ORDER SOMETHING.

When you are using a restaurant's building, table, wait staff, utilities, glassware, and/or paper goods, it is just not good form to order *"a glass of water, please."* (Not to mention, it drives me absolutely crazy.) Even if your stomach is a jumble of nerves, order a cup of tea, a soft drink, a bagel, toast, a cup of soup, SOMETHING! If your appointment is over the lunch hour, order lunch. If you have been invited for dinner, order dinner. If unsure what to order, take your cue from what your interviewer orders.

If you eat only a third of your food or order a very light portion, that's acceptable. I often bring a half-order of untouched food home from an interview because conversation gets in the way of eating.

3. AVOID THE MOST EXPENSIVE ITEMS ON THE MENU.
    Yes, you must eat. No, you do not need to dine on the sumptuous surf-and-turf plate. Ordering the priciest entree at your interviewer's expense may be viewed as a deliberate disregard of financial considerations; not desirable in a potential employee.

I **once invited** *a prospective candidate to a mid-range restaurant for lunch. I ordered a sandwich. My candidate ordered an appetizer, then a steak, followed by a dessert. Upon finishing his three-course feast, he quickly excused himself from the interview, admitting to having no intention of making a job change in the foreseeable future. Since wasted meetings are job hazards intrinsic to the recruitment business, I rarely complain about such a circumstance. But this candidate's blatant exploitation of my time and expense, following a deliberate misrepresentation of his interests, really put me over the edge. Suffice it to say, his "free" lunch cost this candidate any hope of a future job referral or recommendation from me. By the way, I still remember his name after all these years - and not in a good way.*

4. AVOID ALCOHOLIC BEVERAGES.
    Even if it is 5:00 somewhere; even if your interviewer orders a beer; stick to a soft drink. You need a job more than you need the beer. An exception can be made at a social-type group interview in the late stages of the interview process. If everyone at the table is enjoying a pre-dinner cocktail, order a single drink, preferably beer or wine. If you know that one drink has you singing, telling dumb jokes, or sharing anecdotes about your teenage crime spree, avoid alcohol altogether.

5. AVOID FOUR COURSES.

   Unless your interviewer places the order for extras, stick to one course. Try the stuffed squash blossom appetizer and/or the decadent white chocolate cheesecake at your own expense.

6. REMEMBER THE TABLE MANNERS YOUR MAMA TAUGHT YOU.

   Chew with mouth closed. Finish chewing before speaking. Do not attack your food like a wolf which hasn't eaten in a few days. Napkin on lap. Small bites. Inside voice. You remember.

7. AVOID SPAGHETTI...

   ...and ribs. Shy away from any menu item that demands multiple napkins or unusual utensils like chopsticks. Some of the best meals in the world involve a bit of a mess right down to the licking of each of your fingers, but are not recommended for an interview. If you are thinking, *"fingers or fork?"* as you order an item, the answer is, order something else. Fried chicken is not user-friendly.

8. BE COURTEOUS TO WAITERS AND WAITRESSES.

   The way you treat your servers will be seen as a good indicator of how you will treat your co-workers and staff.

9. SAY *"THANK YOU."*

   Thank the person picking up the tab, even if you feel the food was bad and the interview was a complete waste of your time.

   The bottom line is, neither what you eat nor how you eat should become an issue in evaluating your candidacy.

---THE TEAM INTERVIEW: THREE VS. YOU---

You may encounter a situation in which you are interviewed by several representatives of a company gathered around the desk or conference table. The team interview can create some confusion, because often little or no coordination has gone into the interviewers' respective lines of questioning. Additionally, the interviewers may have dissimilar personalities, perform unrelated roles in the company, and express seemingly contradictory expectations. Sound like fun?

Here are a few guidelines for a team interview situation.

Tips for Team Interviews

1. REMEMBER NAMES.

Make sure to memorize the names and positions of each of your interviewers. If necessary, jot down this information on a sheet of paper and place it discreetly in front of you. This will help you to formulate answers that relate to each individual's objectives and interests. Address your interviewers by name when leaving the interview and when sending thank-you notes.

Your interviewers for today will be Herbert Adams, Adam Harvey, Hector Alvarez, and Harold Andrzejewski

2. TREAT EACH INTERVIEWER EQUALLY.

A few months ago, I participated in an interview which included the local general manager of a subsidiary of a nationwide company and a corporate controller. My candidate took an immediate liking to the local manager, answering her questions with enthusiasm. This candidate seemed much less inclined to address the issues of the corporate controller, sometimes treating him as an annoyance. This behavior by the candidate was noticeable to the local manager, the corporate controller, and to me. It was deemed offensive enough to disqualify the candidate from further consideration.

It is always unwise to play favorites during a team interview, even if one of the interviewers in the room will potentially become your direct superior. Treat each individual in the room equally and with respect.

3. MAKE EYE CONTACT.

Make direct, unwavering eye contact with each interviewer when he or she is speaking to you or asking a question. When answering a question, your primary focus should be on the questioner, although you may make brief eye contact with the other interviewers during your answer. An interviewer's body language or facial expression can tell you if you are making points with one person while crashing with another. You may want to follow up with a question to clarify a possible disconnect with any one of the interviewers.

4. DIRECT QUESTIONS TO EACH INTERVIEWER.

Directing questions toward each interviewer will win you points in the follow-up meeting. Try to ask questions that relate specifically to each interviewer's function.

---MARATHON INTERVIEWING: YOU VS. YAWNS---

In an effort to make the most of a candidate's valuable time and/or absence from work, many companies will schedule a series of meetings with multiple decision-makers over the course of a morning, an afternoon, or even a full day. These meetings can prove to be grueling for a candidate, who is expected to be fresh and impressive for each successive interview session. The fourth interviewer of the day has no way of knowing how perky and intelligent you appeared three hours earlier if his only exposure includes a nodding head and stifled yawns.

*M*y *daughter experienced* a marathon interview session while seeking her first position following college graduation. The advertising agency packed eight interviews into a six-hour period, including one which the interviewer conducted while sitting on an exercise ball. My daughter recalls that little or no effort had gone into planning and coordinating the interviews, so she essentially presented and received the same information eight times in a row. It was truly déjà vu all over again and over again and over again.

Nothing I can say will make a marathon interview day as pleasant as a walk in the park, but there are a few ways in which you can make the day easier on yourself.

Tips for Marathon Interviews

1. ARRIVE EARLY.

Be sure to allow enough travel time to permit a few minutes of relaxation and mental composure before you begin your long day. Visit the restroom; run a comb through your hair; refresh your make-up; glance at your notes about the company; review the names of your interviewers. Enter your first interview feeling calm and confident and hope that sets the tone for your day.

2.   BE AWARE OF YOUR OWN METABOLISM.

If you need a cup of coffee in the morning, make sure you get it before you embark on a long series of interviews. If, on the other hand, coffee causes you frequent trips to the restroom, avoid coffee and select small amounts of water instead. A cookie or mint or granola bar between interview sessions can help satisfy mid-morning hunger pangs and provide a little energy boost. If your marathon interview day includes lunch, eat lightly to minimize afternoon sluggishness.

3.   SHAKE HANDS AND MAKE EYE CONTACT AT THE BEGINNING AND END OF EACH SUCCESSIVE INTERVIEW.

Begin and end each interview as if it is your only interview of the day.

4.   MEMORIZE NAMES AND TITLES.

In most cases, the company will have provided you an interview schedule, complete with names and titles. Memorize this list or keep it with you for easy reference. If an agenda is not forthcoming, write your interviewer's name down on a pad of paper you carry with you to your interviews. You can also ask for a business card although some interviewers may not be able to provide one.

5.   USE BREAKS BETWEEN INTERVIEWS WISELY.

Occasionally candidates are ushered from one office to the next with no in-between time. Do not hesitate to ask for a chance to use the restroom between sessions if you need it. Preoccupation with your biological needs cannot help but detract from your upcoming interview performance. If the break between interview sessions is ten or fifteen minutes, do not waste those minutes. Review your research, write up a few notes from your most recent session, refresh your appearance, or even step outside for some fresh air, if that is an option.

6. IF YOU ARE INVITED TO LUNCH, ACCEPT.

    If your interview marathon includes morning and afternoon sessions, you will probably be invited to lunch with one or more of your interviewers. Even though you might trade your left arm for the opportunity of being off-stage for a while, accept the invitation. Regard it as a chance to make personality points with those who will be deciding your future in short order. If you decline a proffered lunch invitation, you might as well go home, as your chances of being hired may have declined to zero. Refer to the previous section regarding interviewing over food.

7. ASK PERTINENT QUESTIONS OF EACH INTERVIEWER.

    Questions are indicative of energy and curiosity. An intelligent question can demonstrate that your mind is active, in addition to deflecting the focus of the interview from you to your interviewer for a brief moment. Do not worry about asking the same question that you have previously asked a different interviewer. Chances are the answers you receive will reflect a slightly different perspective. DO worry about asking the same question twice to a single interviewer. (Near the end of a long day, it could happen.)

8. FOCUS-FOCUS-FOCUS

    I cannot give you a magic solution to keep your concentration level high, only the advice that it is as important to be as focused at 2:00 pm as you were at 9:00 am. Remember, each interviewer has only his or her hour of interview time on which to base a hiring decision that will determine your future. So sit up straight, open your eyes and focus.

9. SEND OR E-MAIL A PERSONAL THANK-YOU TO EACH INTERVIEWER.

10. BEWARE OF THE VETO

The more individuals you meet throughout the day, the greater the chance that you just will not "click" with one of your interviewers. Keep in mind that you do not have the luxury of writing off a single interviewer you don't like. You must treat each interviewer as if he or she is the most pleasant person you have met all day. It may not require a complete consensus to get you hired; but you can be sure that one loud NO vote will get you eliminated from consideration.

---INTERVIEW BY SUBORDINATES: YOU VS. THE INMATES---

On rare occasions, a client will express the wish to have a candidate meet members of his or her future staff before a final hiring decision is made. I generally discourage such a meeting, seeing it as a situation holding huge potential for complications such as:

- If a hiring executive has already reached a decision on a candidate, is that position going to be changed by the opinions of the staff?
- Will members of the staff be unified in their opinions?
- If the hiring executive ignores the opinions of the staff, will it cause dissension?
- If the candidate is hired over the staff's objections, will that candidate be faced with the burden of overcoming their animosity?

Nevertheless, you may be asked to participate in an interview with members of your future staff as a prerequisite to being hired. If you face such a prospect, here are a few suggestions.

Tips for Interviews by Subordinates

1. BE FRIENDLY AND RESPECTFUL.

    This is not the time to put on a display of toughness, lay out demands or set rules. Remember – YOU HAVE NOT BEEN HIRED YET! Your goal is to gain favor among your future co-workers; not to become the subject of scathing water cooler conversations.

2. ASK QUESTIONS.

    Ask questions about what resources the staff is lacking, what problems they are facing, and what input they have to offer. This demonstrates your openness and empathy and can also reveal troublesome circumstances that await you in this role. This may be a learning opportunity that can assist in your decision-making process.

3. SPEAK GENERALLY, NOT SPECIFICALLY.

    Recounting stories that demonstrate your strict management style may be desirable in an interview with company executives; but these stories have the potential to cause trouble when told to future subordinates. Specifically avoid questions about your involvement in terminations, demotions, downsizing or conflicts. In general terms, convey a desire to be fair, helpful, and appreciative of your staff - because you are nice!

4. DEFER TO THE COMPANY LINE.

    When asked specifically how you would handle issues such as arrival times, overtime, internet usage, etc., the simplest answer is *"I will follow company guidelines for dealing with that situation."*

---SUMMARY---

At some point in a lengthy job search, you may experience an extra-challenging interview situation such as interviewing over food; the team interview; the marathon interview; and/or the interview by future subordinates. These types of interviews have the potential to be both enjoyable and rewarding, but they also present interesting opportunities for error. All you can do is execute your interview plan and hope for the best.

INTERVIEW MASTER

Candidate:
Thanks so much for lunch, Bob. I really enjoyed it.

Interviewer:
I did too, Katie. It was nice to get to know you in a relaxed setting. I'm going to recommend that you come to our office next week and meet a few more people.

Chapter 13

Bad Acts and Bad Actors:
Common Interview Flaws

INTERVIEW DISASTER

Interviewer:
Can you tell me a little about your experience at BBetterBank?

Candidate:
I'd rather not.

What happens when a top-rated candidate becomes an exceptionally bad actor in an interview setting? Answer: A second-tier candidate walks away with the job and the top-rated candidate walks away with nothing to show for the experience but a shredded position description and a bruised ego.

You need not deliver an Oscar-caliber performance to succeed at a job interview, but you do have to be a performer of sorts. When the interviewer appears in the doorway and invites you in, you must assume that the spotlight is upon you, the curtain has risen, and you are center stage. You must now perform as though your livelihood depends on it…because, of course, it does.

Unfortunately, performance and presentation skills do not come as naturally to some as they do to others. In the interview scenario, many candidates struggle with the fine line between articulating their strengths and outright bragging. Some tend to speak in mind-numbing monotones. Some talk too much or too softly or too little. Some laugh at inappropriate times. Others have trouble staying on point or even in the vicinity of point. There are manners of interviewing that can superimpose the scarlet letter A for "Annoying" over every impressive credential a candidate has earned. And unfortunately, once an interviewer has been alienated by a candidate's interview style, show time is over and the curtain drops on the opportunity in question.

I once worked for a client who scribbled red flags on his legal pad as candidates attempted to answer his questions. Red flags were not a good sign. I cringed as I saw pages rapidly filling up with red ink. Among the red flags he assigned during one interview was one for repeated use of the common term, "at the end of the day." While there was nothing lacking in the candidate's credentials, and nothing intrinsically offensive about the phrase "at the end of the day," hearing it for the seventeenth time in an hour simply annoyed my client. At the end of the day, that's what was important.

Before anxiety rears its ugly head, let me reassure you that no reasonable interviewer expects a candidate to possess the smooth magnetism of a successful politician.

Most positions don't require magnetism. Most interviewers don't have any desire to be magnetized. But they do want to be able to extract certain information from you without using a pry bar, and they do want to like you.

When I initially meet and screen a candidate, I may become aware that the candidate exhibits one or several shortcomings relating to communication style. If the shortcomings are major and beyond repair, I may choose to eliminate the candidate from further consideration or I may refer him or her to a career coach (suggestion not always received with gratitude). But if the shortcomings are minor, I generally endeavor to help the candidate make some performance adjustments before sending him or her forward in the interview process. While I cannot undo a personality trait that has taken a lifetime to develop, I can try to warn a candidate about an unusual mannerism, an annoying habit, or a vocal quirk.

Harry Callahan, also known as Dirty Harry, said it best in the movie Magnum Force: *"A man's got to know his limitations."* [2] Becoming aware of one's own limitations is the first step to conquering them. But sometimes it is easier to recognize our own faults when we see them in others. With that in mind, I am going to introduce you to some "bad actors." These fictional creations are composites of real-life, high-level, professional candidates I have encountered in my career as a headhunter. As you read, keep in mind that these candidates missed out on unique opportunities not because of poor qualifications, but because of poor interviewing skills. One or more of these characters just might have a resemblance to you. If the shoe fits……..

---TALK-YOU-TO-DEATH TOM---

You have all met Tom. He's the one who answers a straightforward, 20-second question with an eight-minute, meandering monologue. He happily provides unrelated details, gives superfluous examples, re-plays entire conversations, references unfamiliar names (*"I am sure you know Bill Whistledixie - you must!"*), and re-lives experiences that occurred fourteen years in the past. While detailed examples often add credibility to a candidate's presentation, too much of a good thing can be a very bad thing.

Chances are, I will have noticed Tom's propensity to prattle during our first encounter, by phone or face-to-face. If the trait is extreme, I may disqualify Tom from further evaluation because of my own impatience or because I foresee daggers flying at me from my client's eyes as Tom talks…and talks…and talks. But if the unfortunate trait seems to be manageable, I will try to manage it through coaching and interview preparation. Here are some reminders (note the clever S-H-O-R-T mnemonic device) if you suspect that Tom is alive and talking in you:

- **SIGNALS.** Watch for signals from your audience. These include checking the blackberry, consulting the watch, yawning, and Twittering. My family has a one-word signal for too-long monologues: EGO for Eyes-Glazing-Over.
- **HIGH POINTS.** Do not provide unnecessary names and details in your answers.
- **OUTLINE.** Before you begin to answer a question, make a mental outline of where you are headed. Try not to venture too far from your outline.
- **RELEVANCE.** Confine storytelling to experiences that emphasize the benefits you can bring to the client. You are not at the interview to deliver comedy or engage in cocktail party banter.
- **TWO MINUTES.** I've mentioned the two-minute rule before. In your mind, visualize a two-minute timer. When the sand has run out, it is time to let the interviewer back into the conversation.

---COVERT KATE---

At the opposite end of the communication spectrum, we have Covert Kate. Kate may have been trained in the CIA or she is just concise to a fault. She answers every question in 15 words or less, which may result in a very brief interview with a very unsatisfactory ending.

*O**n one occasion,** when I was recruiting candidates for a controller position at an out-of-state location, I scheduled an initial interview with a woman who appeared on paper to be a nice fit. In our initial phone conversation, she was very reserved but provided enough information to get to the next level.*

We met at a casual restaurant over lunch, perhaps the longest lunch I have ever endured. This woman avoided polite niceties, withheld information as if she were a suspect in a criminal interrogation, and provided me with little more than her name, rank and serial number. It was impossible to get a handle on what her responsibilities were, what she actually did or what her accomplishments were. Personal safety and security should always be kept in the forefront of your thinking. But once you have made the choice to enter the job market and have agreed to meet a recruiter, you should expect to dole out some information. Once you send out the first resume, assume that your confidentiality has been somewhat compromised and start forking over the facts.

If you have covert tendencies, I encourage you to think of yourself as an active participant in your interviews rather than just an answerer of questions. Force yourself to ask questions, relate experiences, discuss and verbally back up the skills you claim to have.

When you answer each question, consider the difference between a penciled stick man drawing and a digital photo. It is wonderful to respond to a question that, oh yes, you have worked with the operations people at the plant. It is more memorable to cite a real instance in which your relationship with the plant personnel resulted in positive results for your employer. Similarly, if you claim to have worked with tight deadlines, describe an occasion in which you and your staff worked around the clock to have a document at the printer by 7:00 a.m. when the printer opened the shop.

---GOOD OLE' PAL PAUL---

Occasionally an interviewer and interviewee may share a significant number of acquaintances and some history. The candidate may be a referral from a mutual friend. The interviewer and candidate may have attended the same high school or college. Or the two may have worked in the same industry for years, been members of the same professional associations, dealt with the same suppliers, or even worked for the same terrible boss. Common ground is a good thing, serving to defuse natural interview tensions, but can turn out badly if the interviewee becomes too comfortable or familiar during the interview.

W *orking for a client with a small semi-rural location in the Midwest, I was able to recruit five candidates for the assigned position. One of the candidates lived in close proximity to the company and had worked with a well-known competitor for many years. He entered the interview and immediately began directing conversation toward mutual acquaintances and the state of the local industry scene, instead of offering useful information about his career background. The candidate never detailed what he was capable of based upon HIS individual accomplishments. Instead, he wasted the opportunity to "sell" his achievements and ended up losing the position to an equally qualified candidate.*

When you are interviewing, remember to maintain a professional distance between yourself and your interviewer. You are not seeking to establish a buddy relationship; you are looking to get hired. If you share acquaintances or friends or history, it is advisable to avoid any lengthy discussion of those relationships during your job interview, for fear of appearing to use those relationships to unfair advantage. Instead, focus on what you have done and what you, personally, can bring to the position in question. Common acquaintances and shared experience are nice. Even nicer is the way you saved your former employer time and dollars through implementing more efficient methods.

---NOTE-ORIOUS NICOLE---

To say that Nicole has prepared for her interview is an understatement. Nicole has read multiple books on interviewing, analyzed her strengths and weaknesses, and composed numerous answers to possible interview questions in her head and on paper. She brings her notes with her and refers to them constantly during the course of the interview. Instead of answering questions thoughtfully, she uses her notes as a crutch, referring to them for even obvious answers.

*O**ne of my former candidates,** a female, arrived at her interview impeccably dressed and, by all appearances, well-prepared for her interview. Upon taking her seat at the interview table, she opened her portfolio, removed a sheet of paper, and placed it directly in front of her. I observed that the paper was completely covered in handwritten notes written so small as to be unreadable. This document, once called a crib sheet, would have been a source of pride to a student trying to cheat on an exam.*

As we proceeded through the interview, my candidate referred to her notes to answer even the most basic of questions such as names of companies where she had been employed. Instead of a back-and-forth exchange of information, the interview came to resemble a test of sorts (the open book variety) with little revealed about the candidate's ability to think and react in a stressful situation. Or maybe a lot was revealed. This candidate did not win the position.

If a few written notes increase your confidence, by all means bring them to your interview. Certainly, a copy of your resume may be a handy tool, especially when you are asked for specific dates or details of your background. But it is better to refer to written notes only occasionally, instead maintaining eye contact and conversation flow with others in the room. It is your career we are discussing. Remembering the basics of your resume should not be that difficult and you should know them cold.

Failing to remember a detail or two from your background will not be held against you in your interview. Establishing a friendly, personal rapport with your interviewer will compensate for your inability to answer each question to the second decimal place.

---SHARE-IT-ALL SEAN---

Sean is a gregarious, likable guy whose nature is to share personal stories and cultivate friendships. We all want to have a neighbor like Sean. And most interviewers will enjoy interviewing Sean.

But the sharing of too much personal information in an interview situation is risky. Every interviewer brings a set of personal values and prejudices to the interview setting, which may not be in complete harmony with yours. The more information you provide about your personal life, the greater the opportunity that your interviewer will find something not to like.

Do you have eleven children? That is wonderful, but some interviewer might wonder if your large family will distract you from your heavy workload or create a financial burden for you.

Are you recently divorced? Your potential employer might have concerns about your emotional stability and financial situation.

Do you visit the casino every Friday night? You may be a responsible gambler, but don't gamble a future opportunity by discussing your winnings at a job interview.

I *n filling a controller position* *for one of my clients, I presented a young man who was an ideal candidate. He had the perfect combination of experience and education to enable him to succeed in this position, and easily proceeded to the second and third interview. At the final interview, in the process of thrashing out the details of his likely job offer, there was a discussion regarding his start date. The company proposed the Tuesday after Labor Day. My candidate requested that the date be deferred until Wednesday, because he generally "tied one on" with family and friends on Labor Day. Partying with friends on a summer holiday is not uncommon, but basing his career future on his hangover raised some questions about the candidate's work ethic and his judgment. After a short discussion, the company decided to move on to a different candidate.*

During the average interview, it is common to mention your spouse, your child, your childhood, or a recent event in your life. To avoid any such conversation might appear awkward and unfriendly; perhaps even secretive. However, providing too many personal details, without the perspective of your positive business performance as a foundation, can be risky. Tread this line carefully. When it comes to your personal life, the interviewer is not entitled to more than the very basics. Save personal sharing for after you have been hired.

---SUMMARY---

The above fictional characters are composites of real-life candidates who have lost opportunities because of poor interview skills. If you believe or have been advised that you exhibit flaws in your personal presentation, do not despair. Self-awareness and self-discipline can solve any number of presentation problems. For more serious problems, I recommend that candidates might want to consult a career coach, who has been trained to identify idiosyncrasies and help individuals resolve them.

Let me assure you once again that no interviewer expects perfection. Be yourself, be confident about who you are, and be enthusiastic about your future and about each opportunity. A positive and optimistic demeanor will outweigh most mistakes.

INTERVIEW MASTER

Candidate:

I've been talking for several minutes now, so let me take a break. Do you have any questions?

Chapter 14

Interview Aftermath:
Writing-Waiting-Worrying

INTERVIEW DISASTER

Interviewer:

Ashley in HR, please...Hello, Ashley. I just wanted to let you know that I really liked Charlie Gray when we interviewed him for the financial analyst position last week, but he's called me twice every day since the interview...he's coming across as very "high maintenance." I am going to pass on him. Please send him an e-mail, a letter, something as soon as you can! Get him off my back!

Your interview is over. Your preparation and research paid off, enabling you to display your knowledge of the industry and the company. You anticipated and prepared for your interview questions and answered them, providing details and examples from your background. Your performance was, in your humble opinion, a bases-loaded home run. What now?

Now you treat yourself to a double cheeseburger with fries and a shake, or a Chicago style hot dog, a soak in the hot tub at the gym, or, my personal self-congratulatory celebration, a martini with two olives and a twist (but only if it is afternoon somewhere).

Yes, you deserve a short break in which to lower your heart rate down to a normal range. But after the break, you need to finish the job you have started. Following your interview, there remain several small but very important tasks to be completed. These must-do items are not deal-makers but, in a tight competition, could be deal-breakers. Omitting the proper interview follow-up procedure could make the difference between *"When can you start?"* and *"Next candidate, please."*

---TAKE THE PARKING LOT TEST---

Immediately after your interview and before aforementioned martini, I recommend taking what I call "the parking lot test," an on-the-spot analysis of your reaction to the interview. I have found the parking lot test to be a frequently accurate measure of a candidate's potential happiness in a given situation. The reason for its accuracy is its immediacy. Time allows you to cast a different light on your interview; a light that may not reflect truth.

The parking lot test is brief and revealing. Four questions and done. No one will know the results but you. I love the test, because I created the test. Here are the four questions:

The Parking Lot Test

⇒ THE ENVIRONMENT QUESTION:
As you approach your automobile in the parking lot adjoining the interview site, take a look at the building you just left (assuming you are at the offices of the potential employer and not the airport). Your brain should be brimming with information about this company and this position. Does looking back at the office building cause a sense of impending doom? Can you picture yourself arriving here to work every day? Do you wish you could stay and start work right now? How was the commute? Three-plus hours in the car every day will wear down even a stock car driver in a very short period of time.

⇒ THE PEOPLE QUESTION:
As you sit in your car, while your memory is still fresh, ask yourself, what is your instinct saying to you about the people you met today? Can you envision any/all of these people as potential friends or co-workers? Does a specific person you met today have to leave the company in order for the working environment to be acceptable? Trust yourself. Your instincts on this are right most of the time

⇒ THE JOB CONTENT QUESTION:
Is the content of the job going to fulfill your intellectual needs now and in the future? Is this job a move forward or a step backward in your career? Is it a good positioning move for the future? Is this job going to be a ten-hour-a-day firefight, or eight hours (counted in six-minute segments) of mind-numbing boredom? Remember that the ultimate mind-numbing existence is called jail. Will coming to work be like coming to jail? Will this job provide sufficient challenges? Is this job something you are able to do?

⇒ THE GUT REACTION QUESTION:
If your answers to the previous questions are relatively positive, you can proceed to the final question, which is really a composite of the preceding questions. When you think about the possibility of landing this job, does it put a smile on your face? Are you excited? Does your gut reaction feel like a red light or a green light? If you are experiencing nothing but anticipation and enthusiasm, that's bright green. If you feel an element of doubt, that's a yellow or red light, possibly even a roadblock.

And that's the entire test! Simplistic, maybe, but a quick self-examination when your reactions are true and untarnished by time, is invaluable. The process may give you the confidence to proceed with a yes or no decision regarding a particular position. If nothing else, the parking lot test will force you to pause from the intense interview process to gather your thoughts while your recollections are still fresh. This is when you see the situation as it is, without the enhancement of mental justification.

The point of this exercise is to trust your first instincts. If the commute seems intolerable; if you have taken an instant dislike to someone you just met; if the job is an unwarranted step backward in your career; if the job demands exceed your abilities; if the working hours do not fit your lifestyle; this is the time to swallow the bitter reality pill. It is much better and easier to walk away from an unaccepted opportunity now than to escape from a miserable job three months from now.

On the other hand, if your parking lot test has revealed a gleaming green light, proceed without hesitation to accomplish the final steps of the interview process. Remember that your interview ain't over 'til the fat lady sings and the last thank-you note is written.

---PROVIDING FEEDBACK:
RECRUITER AS INTERMEDIARY---

If you were recruited directly by the hiring company, there is no requirement to offer verbal feedback to the company until you receive a call-back. In fact, there is an unwritten rule that you do not phone your interviewer until at least one week past the interview. Follow this rule. Be patient. Wait.

However, if you were presented by an external recruiter, you should contact that recruiter with your feedback as soon as possible, preferably within hours of the interview. I can assure you he will be waiting for your call and that his client will be waiting for his call. This is the point where your recruiter can be of great service to you, acting as your liaison with the hiring company.

Provide as much feedback as you can to the recruiter. As you describe whom you met, the length of your meetings, the questions you received, the high and low points, and your current interest level, the recruiter will begin to develop a sense of how well or poorly your interview went. Like a mechanic diagnosing a car in need of repair, a recruiter is experienced in diagnosing interview results. Each piece of information can suggest something positive or negative. For instance, if you were scheduled to meet one person and ended up meeting four, this could be a very good sign. Conversely, if you were scheduled to meet three and were dismissed after the first meeting, it would be a matter for concern. The recruiter may be able to obtain unvarnished feedback which will be beneficial to you, no matter the outcome.

If you are anxious about some aspect of your interview performance or have developed further questions since the interview, share your concerns with the recruiter. He will probably have a direct pipeline to the client for feedback about you and from you. He will be able ask the interviewer about your status, identify questions and/or issues on the part of the company and, in some cases, be able to repair minor presentation flaws. Armed with your impression of the interview, the recruiter will be able to trumpet your interest. If the company has a specific concern, the recruiter may be able to address it on your behalf.

You may have been told that there is no such thing as a dumb question. That would be incorrect. But here's the good news. Recruiters are excellent soundboards for dumb questions. If you wisely avoided asking a sensitive (or dumb) question during your interview, you should feel free to ask the recruiter after the interview when it cannot be indelibly held against you. If the recruiter sees that the question has some merit, he/she can ask it on your behalf. Your recruiter potentially will wear the egg. You will continue to look like a genius.

You can see how working with a recruiter has its advantages. (Remarked the headhunter.)

A *family friend* is currently engaged in a job search. *Recently, she participated in a series of interviews at the same company with progressively higher-level decision makers. After her fourth (yes fourth) visit, she waited anxiously for over a week, receiving no word from the company regarding her fate. Having worked through a headhunter relating to previous opportunities, she lamented that she felt very frustrated at the lack of access to feedback that is customarily provided by an external recruiter.*

---THANK-YOU NOTES---

You must send a written thank-you note to each individual at the company who was involved in your interviewing process. In addition to demonstrating basic good manners, this thank-you note serves to confirm your interest in the position or advise the company that you do not wish to proceed further. Yes, you must send a thank-you note even if you have decided not to pursue the position. Your sincere thank-you note leaves an open door behind you, should another position in the company arise.

The thank-you note process begins during your interviews with gathering contact information on each person you need to thank. If you were not able to do this over the course of your interview via exchange of business cards or e-mail addresses, a phone call to the receptionist to collect such information is appropriate. Make every effort to send your note(s) within 24 hours. If you are thanking several individuals, I suggest a personalized note versus sending the exact same note to each. In today's environment, e-mail notes appear to be acceptable to most people. If you are vying for a higher level role, I suggest the more formal approach of a mailed letter on high quality stationary.

The thank-you note should be a brief expression of appreciation for the time spent and an acknowledgement of your continuing interest (or lack thereof) in the opportunity at hand. You can introduce information that would be positive to your case that was not addressed during your meeting. But this is not an opportunity to resell what you have already presented and should not be used as such. The more your note personally targets each recipient, the better.

Following are two examples of acceptable thank-you notes for a candidate interested in pursuing a position.

The first example is suitable for just about any role and suitable for e-mail.

Dear John:

I very much enjoyed meeting with you today. Thanks for your time.

It appears that your career at NuCo has been exciting and successful. Based upon what you shared with me, I would be very interested in becoming a member of the team.

I look forward to the next step in the process.

Sincerely,

Jim Donnelley

Example 2 is appropriate for a higher level role. A note such as this can be sent via e-mail if the recipient appears to be e-mail savvy. There are some executives out there who do not touch a computer or own a Blackberry. This is a judgment call.

Dear Bill:

Our meeting today was enjoyable and very insightful. I appreciate your time and the opportunity to discuss the strategic plan for NuCo.

From our discussion, it appears that you have assembled some outstanding team members. I can visualize my experience in our industry having a very positive impact on the team's ability to achieve the stated goals in the short term and long term.

As you move forward in the decision-making process, I want you to know that I am very interested in the opportunity and would welcome your continued interest.

Sincerely,

Mike Doherty

Example 3 is a note you might write if you have decided against pursuing the position.

Dear Allison:

It was a pleasure meeting you yesterday and learning about the Marketing Coordinator role at BizCo. Although BizCo and the position sound very attractive, I have decided that the position is not the right fit for me at this point in my career.

Thank you for your time. I truly enjoyed our discussion and wish you the best of luck in your search efforts.

Sincerely,

Jason Kramer

A thank-you note will not miraculously resurrect a death-by-interview. But if you are in the running for a position, a timely note can make a difference. One candidate I worked with won a job offer by sending a thank-you note when the other candidate did not. All other things being equal, the thank-you note could become a factor.

---REFERENCES---

Unless this is your first job out of college, you can assume that references will be requested following a late-stage interview and before any offer is made. Most employers want to speak to your previous supervisors and co-workers to confirm their observations and perceptions. When professionally done, references can be very useful not only in confirming a good impression, but may also provide insight that can help an employer maximize your performance in the new environment.

Usually, the application process will require that you list several references, provide contact information, and give permission for the employer to contact the individuals. The individuals listed should include at least one supervisor and a meaningful co-worker. When completing any application that requests references, you should make it clear that no individuals are to be contacted for reference purposes unless you have been notified. This way, you can safeguard your privacy, as well as saving your friends and colleagues from wasteful and time-consuming verbal exercises unless you have serious intentions of pursuing a job

You must always advise individuals when you wish to use their names as references. This will require informing them that you are looking for a new job and asking them if they feel comfortable providing information about you to a potential employer. Some people will decline for one reason or another, which may never be revealed to you. Accept it and move on. It is far better for an individual to decline than to give a negative or lukewarm reference. Others will enthusiastically agree. Never list an individual as a reference unless you feel absolutely certain that the individual will be positive.

It is my practice to delay contacting any individuals for references until my client has expressed a very serious interest in the candidate. At this point, I advise the candidate of my plans and request that the candidate notify each individual that I will be calling. By waiting until late in the process, I am assured that both the company and the candidate have serious intentions about moving forward before I jeopardize the candidate's privacy relating to his or her job search.

*S**ome years back,** I had a neighbor who was a sales executive with an international pharmaceutical distribution company. One day while I was mowing my lawn, Bill approached me to ask my opinion on a legal matter.*

It seems that a former direct report had listed Bill as a reference without his permission. When a recruiter called him to ask a few questions, Bill was stunned and told the recruiter why. Of all the employees who had ever worked for him, this woman was the most high-maintenance, pain-in-the-backside he could recall. Bill added that he could not believe that she would list him as a reference, particularly without asking him. For reasons I cannot explain, Bill chose to continue speaking in brutally honest fashion.

Several weeks later, he received a cease-and-desist letter from a west coast law firm indicating that legal action was forthcoming. The candidate had not been hired by the prospective employer and was told that Bill's negative reference was the reason. The candidate was contemplating suing for damages.

In this case, both parties were dead wrong. First, the candidate should have contacted Bill to ask if he would act as a favorable reference. Presumably, he would have declined. Second, when the recruiter called for the reference, Bill should have politely refused to engage in conversation.

---THE WAITING GAME---

After you have contacted your recruiter (if applicable) with feedback, written the required thank-you notes, and contacted your references if necessary, you can put your feet up and relax, comfortable in the knowledge that you have done all you can to win the desired position.

Now comes what can be the most frustrating part of the post-interview process for many candidates, the waiting. Waiting may be easy if you are happily employed in a paying job; less so if you are watching cable news shows all day with no paycheck in the foreseeable future.

What amount of waiting time is standard?

Throughout my career, I have been able to provide most of my candidates with a client's decision within a week's time. But in today's listless economy, it seems to me that some decisions are being made with the speed of a glacier slogging through an icy sea. I have experienced silent periods of several weeks waiting for a thumbs-up or thumbs-down verdict on a candidate. If I am growing impatient, I can only assume that my candidate is pacing the floor at 3 a.m.

So how long must a candidate wait before initiating post-interview contact?

If you are working with a recruiter, it is acceptable to call the recruiter for an update every few days. Based upon the recruiter's relationship with his client, he may know what is occurring at the company and when a decision can be expected. Or he may be as much in the dark as you are. It is important to let your recruiter make the feedback requests to the company, as the company has hired him to function as its point of contact with candidates. Remember that even a recruiter cannot serve up a final decision before it has been made, but he can and should keep you apprised of any developments.

If you are dealing directly with the company, the waiting period question is more difficult. I suggest that if no contact has been established for a full week from the date of your interview, it is appropriate to send an e-mail to your interviewer or your human resources contact at the company. The e-mail should be brief and polite, expressing your continued interest in the position and requesting an update on the status of the decision-making process. In most cases, this will initiate a response updating your status. Unfortunately, that response may be "still undecided" or even worse.

> *If your wait begins to drag out over several weeks, you can begin to assume one of three things, all bad:*
> - *You are dealing with rude or unprofessional individuals;*
> - *Something major or unexpected is occurring within the company that has delayed the decision-making process; or*
> - *You have somehow slipped through the administrative cracks.*

It has been my experience that you do not have to chase good news. By participating in a job interview, you have earned the right to be notified of whatever decision results from that interview. If a company fails to notify you about interview results, it reveals nothing good about the company.

Once two weeks have passed since your interview date, it is acceptable to make a phone call to your interviewer at the company. If you are unable to reach this individual and your call is not returned after a day or two, try a different point of contact such as another interviewer or someone in the human resources department. If you still do not receive a call-back or any feedback, you must mentally let go of the opportunity, assume the worst and proceed elsewhere with your job search. Never leave more than two phone messages with any one individual, for fear of being seen as a stalker candidate.

The case of the stalker candidate

C ***ontacting a company*** *or even a recruiter too aggressively or too often can win you stalker status and lose a potential job. A few years back, I was able to observe a truly unique example of a job stalker. Let's call her Claire Capelli.*

One of my partners in the search firm had spoken to and established a mentor-type relationship with Claire over the course of several months. He had found her professional skills to be adequate, but her interpersonal skills somewhat flawed, so had not been able to recommend her to a client. The subject of Claire had come up in office conversation several times, most recently during the past week when she had called to tell my partner that she had interviewed at a company for an accounting position. She advised my partner that she felt the interview had gone extremely well, but had not heard from the company since her interview the previous week.

Late on Friday afternoon, my partner received a strange call at the office. It was a very agitated Claire Capelli, calling from... the local police station! Claire, wrongly assuming the best results from her interview, had taken it upon herself to visit the company to begin negotiating her salary and start date. (Claire cannot be faulted for lacking a positive mental attitude.) Within minutes, a startled receptionist politely asked Claire to leave. When Claire persisted in her demands, someone at the company called the police and Claire was carted down to the police station and charged with trespassing.

Did I mention Claire's interpersonal skills were somewhat flawed?

To sum up the general rules of candidate/company contact following an interview for employment when an external recruiter is not involved:

- Positive results from an interview will generally be communicated through a phone call invitation to return to the company, usually within a week of the interview.
- If no phone call or other contact is initiated by the company, following up on a potential opportunity is a normal and acceptable action by the candidate.
- An e-mail request for status after one week followed by a phone call at the two-week mark should result in a status update.
- If no explanation or update has been provided by this time, a candidate must question the wisdom of moving forward with this company and look for other opportunities to pursue.

Over the years, I have experienced a few rare situations in which I was surprised by positive feedback so long after the interview process that I had already advised my candidates to move on without looking back. Some candidates, particularly, unemployed candidates, may be elated with such tardy news; many candidates will have become so disenchanted by the inefficient process and the lack of professionalism that they feel fortunate to have avoided a potentially bad situation.

---SUMMARY---

After your interview is over, several important tasks remain:

- Perform the parking lot test, an on-the-spot analysis of your immediate reactions to help you determine whether or not you want the position;
- Provide your feedback immediately if working with a recruiter;
- Write thank-you notes to each person involved in your interview, even if you have decided not to pursue the opportunity;
- Wait patiently for the results of your interview, following up only after a week to two weeks.

If your interview went well, you should receive positive feedback in somewhat short order, probably via phone. If your interview didn't go so well, you should receive word of negative results via mailed letter or e-mail within approximately two weeks.

As a general rule, and one that consistently guides my actions relating to my candidates and clients, you do not have to chase good news.

INTERVIEW MASTER

Interviewer:

I'm sorry it's been almost a week since your interview. I've been in China and I'm just getting the chance to call you. We were very impressed with your presentation. If you're still interested, we'd like to schedule a second interview later this week.

Candidate:

Thank you. I'd love to pursue the opportunity further.

Chapter 15

Negotiating your Job Offer:
Bucks and Benefits

INTERVIEW DISASTER

Candidate:

   I was hoping for a little better salary.

Interviewer:

   And we were hoping for a little better candidate. Things being what they are, let's all just get happy.

The complete interview cycle, beginning with an unanticipated phone call from a company or recruiter and ending with a much-anticipated phone call or letter from a company or recruiter, can last from several days to many months (in rare cases). Factors that determine the length of the process include scheduling challenges, importance or level of the position, number of candidates being considered, number of individuals involved in decision-making, and the degree of prioritization given to the hire.

   But every series of interviews has one thing in common. In the end, one candidate gets a call extending an offer of employment.

At some point in your job search, perhaps more than once, you will be that candidate. When this happens, you will probably consider yourself lucky.

But luck did not earn this job offer. You did. When you receive an offer of employment, it is because of your hard work, your wise career planning, and your interview preparation and performance. If you were in the right place at the right time, it is because you networked and marketed and put yourself in the right place. Take a few moments to congratulate yourself on your achievement.

Then get back to the task. You're not done yet.

---FALLING IN AND OUT OF LOVE---

An offer of employment is cause for celebration, but also a time for one final session of careful analysis. It can never hurt to take one last look before plunging in headfirst. Not looking, on the other hand, can lead to a chronic headache.

An employer with a job opening can be a seductive suitor, particularly if you are unemployed or unhappy in your current situation. If you "fell in love" early in the interview process, you may have blinded yourself to any negative input that challenged what you wanted to hear; the equivalent of *"Honey, I'm not really twenty-eight,"* or *"Sweetheart, I'm not really a wealthy executive."* When you receive a job offer, it is time to step back and try to take a rational look at whether the object of your pursuit will provide lasting happiness after the heady romance is over.

Just as you presented the truth in a favorable light during your interview "courtship," so did your potential employer. So while nearly all interviewers are truthful, the whole story may be somewhat more elusive. Now that you have received your offer of employment, review the entire interview process from beginning to end for a clue or even an outright admission of reality that you failed to hear. If at some point during the interview process you lost your neutral mindset, it might have kept you from paying heed to information that will now help you to evaluate this opportunity and even negotiate your compensation package.

By the way, if you have become aware that the interview process induces stress, wait until you receive a job offer, the mother of all stress inducers. Prior to this moment in the interview process, you have been able to walk away with no strings attached. Now, feel the strings tightening. Your future hangs on the words you say and the choices you make following your offer of employment.

In this chapter, I will advise you on the nuts and bolts of negotiating a job offer. But before I talk about negotiating a job offer, I want to talk about <u>not</u> negotiating a job offer.

---WALKING AWAY---

It has always been my philosophy that if a candidate is going to walk away from an opportunity, the sooner he or she takes the first footstep on that walk, the better for all involved. The 24 hours following a job offer, while extremely late in the process, represent the last, best chance to walk away from an opportunity leaving few or no burnt bridges behind you. Once you begin the negotiating process, the bridges have been drizzled with gasoline.

> *Let me say this as clearly as I can. Do not begin to negotiate a better offer for a job you do not intend to take.*

A bad job with a higher salary is still a bad job. A micromanaging boss will still be gazing over your shoulder, regardless of your extra week of vacation. If a situation is imperfect or intolerable, recognize it. Acknowledge it. Terminate the process (politely). Walk away.

Note: If you want to witness genuine anger, make an employer jump through hoops to get you a better salary offer and then turn down the job anyway. This has happened and, unfortunately, I can bear witness that foul words were spoken.

A completely different scenario is an exciting, career-boosting job where a small salary or vacation differential is the only obstacle. This is definitely a prospect worth negotiating.

---DELIVERY OF THE OFFER---

Offers can be extended by several methods and by a number of individuals. For example, I, as an external recruiter, am frequently called upon to deliver an offer on behalf of my client. In larger companies, Human Resources professionals often convey offers of employment. Sometimes an eventual direct supervisor may prefer to extend the offer directly to a candidate.

Recruiter-Delivered Offer

When I deliver an offer of employment to a candidate, my client typically has armed me with the following information: base salary amount, potential bonus range, and any other cash compensation options. I am strictly the money messenger. Other than to note that they are part of the offer, I never address any benefit specifics or equity participation matters. These are important issues that must be addressed in detail by appropriate, knowledgeable company representatives. My job is to determine a candidate's acceptance or rejection of the monetary salary offer. If that offer is accepted in principle, I immediately provide the candidate with contact information so that he or she may continue negotiations directly with the company. Generally, the company will arrange to have an explanation of benefits forwarded with a formal offer letter very soon, usually the next day. Equity participation issues are complex and must be addressed formally in writing.

Before we go further, I must provide a word of caution. When I offer a candidate a position, my word is as good as a bar of solid gold. Still, I am only an external recruiter. My word does not carry the weight of the company who will be signing your paychecks. ALWAYS insist on written communication directly from the hiring company before considering a job offered and accepted.

Employer-Delivered Offer

If a Human Resources professional or a hiring representative from the company has extended an employment offer over the phone, this verbal offer is formal and is binding on the company. Still, I recommend that you NEVER resign or make financial commitments based upon your new employment until a formal offer letter is received, confirming the spoken agreement and addressing all aspects of salary, equity participation, and benefits.

When you receive a job offer, it is easy to get carried away with the anticipation of the blissful new future that lies ahead. Slow down. Get your offer in writing. Do not commit to luxury vacation accommodations in Hawaii next winter. Read your offer. Have someone you trust read your offer. It is very appropriate to ask for a day, maybe two, to review the details of your offer. Ask and review.

---TO ASK OR NOT TO ASK – FOR MORE MONEY---

Almost without exception, the first words from a candidate following my delivery of a job offer are *"Is that as high as they will go?"* Regardless of the compensation amount, it seems most candidates are curious as to whether more dollars are on the table.

Asking this question of an external recruiter like me is always acceptable. In cases where the company has indicated to me that it feels extremely generous about its initial offer, I might recommend to the candidate that I not advance the request to my client. But when it appears that some salary negotiation is going to be required to sign, seal and deliver an acceptance of terms, I am certainly willing to bring the matter to the client's attention. Ultimately, the employer and the candidate must come to terms on salary offers and requests, so I am merely a link in the chain of communication.

I suggest that if you are negotiating directly with your prospective employer, you might want to consider carefully any request for more compensation if the company has already offered a significant raise over your most recent salary. By appearing to have unreasonable or insatiable salary demands, you run the risk of alienating your employer before Day One of your tenure on the job. But in the end, you must determine what is acceptable to you.

Let's talk about some ways of negotiating a higher salary.

Negotiating a Higher Salary – Early Career

If you are in the first five or six years of your career, there is likely to be little room for movement with respect to the salary component of your job offer. You can expect to be paid within an established range, based upon your years of experience and your current compensation. In addition, you will likely be offered a standard employee benefits package. Because there are many individuals capable of performing lower level jobs, entry level and low level salaries tend to be somewhat similar across an industry. Yes, you are great at what you do. No, not that great. However, this does not mean you cannot ask for more money. There is no harm in trying.

> *To improve your chances of scoring additional dollars, be ready to offer some form of justification that will advance your cause.*

For instance, your graduate degree or professional certification may warrant additional dollars if it differentiates you from your peers. A suggestion that you plan to enroll in some classes that will enhance your job performance might elicit a small salary increase to offset tuition payments. (Plan to enroll sooner rather than later if you have used this argument.) Fluency in French may make you more valuable than your peers to a company that has a subsidiary in Montreal. C'est bon!

When requesting more salary, do not refer to such things as your difficulties in making the payments on your newly purchased sports car (*"How does my new Accounts Payable Supervisor afford a Bentley?"*) Nor should you mention "cost of living" or "credit card debt." As with every other facet of interviewing, your salary negotiations should be focused on the benefits you can provide to your employer, not vice versa.

An area that may offer you some haggling potential is the bartering of benefits for cash. For instance, if your health care is nicely covered through your spouse's benefit package, you might suggest that you will forego this benefit in lieu of additional cash compensation. I have seen this happen only in closely held, smaller companies where a predetermined benefits package is not standard to all employees. Conversely, I was also part of an offer from a small, European-based company in which everything but a new refrigerator was provided in the benefits package, but there was to be no budging on a below-market salary offer.

If you have expressed some dissatisfaction with your salary offer, but the company has no room to maneuver, a one-time signing bonus may be an option. Signing bonuses are sometimes used by employers to incent an individual to quickly accept a position. They are also used to offset other perceived deficiencies in the offer (company just hired Ozzy Osbourne as CEO). Some signing bonuses are paid immediately while others are held until you reach a specific milestone such as thirty days of employment. If the payment is deferred six months, it is not actually a signing bonus but a convoluted deferred compensation arrangement. In cases where a salary increase is not possible, a signing bonus may be a satisfactory substitute.

Negotiating a Higher Salary – Upper Level Positions

As your career moves up the food chain, your experience portfolio becomes more unique and your compensation options grow accordingly. The final compensation package will be influenced by market conditions, your perceived value to the organization, your level of responsibility, your level of impact on the company's future, peer compensation and of course, your current compensation package. Obviously, negotiation of an offer at this level becomes much more complex.

Some of the additional payment components beyond base salary include but are not limited to:

— Bonus potential,
— Performance objective driven compensation,
— Options/warrants/stock,
— Various insurance products,
— Expense allowances,
— Travel allowances,
— Private club expenses,
— Vacation,
— Company vehicle,
— Relocation expenses,
— Deferred compensation,
— Retirement plans, and/or
— Severance arrangements.

Once multiple factors are involved, it is challenging to evaluate an offer versus your current compensation or versus a competing offer. I spoke to a colleague of mine, a partner in a highly regarded retained firm who has recruited many top level executives, about this issue. He said that an offer reflects the company's vision of your potential based upon your past performance and is tempered by the company's (and your) appetite for risk. He agreed with me that side-by-side analysis of two situations comprised of multiple variables, particularly when one of those variables is outcome-based, can be next to impossible. He shared my belief that there can be no black-and-white, definitive conclusion in such comparisons.

Still, a wise candidate interested in maximizing his or her compensation will make the attempt.

A first step in comparing a job offer versus your current compensation is to write down each component of your current compensation package and try to place a realistic monetary value on that component. The sum of all these components serves as a baseline from which to measure a competing offer.

Next, you should research compensation paid out for similar roles at comparable companies. There are many sources of comparative information. Among these are:

- **PROXY STATEMENTS.** If the company extending your job offer is public and you are at a very high level, the company's proxy statement is a source of such information. Typically, a proxy statement will detail base salary, bonus, stock/option holdings and any significant perks paid to each officer of the company. If you can find a publicly held company that is a competitor to your potential employer, the compensation data will be very helpful to you, once scaled for company size differential.

- **SEARCH PROFESSIONALS.** Experienced executive search professionals who are experts in an industry are also sources of current data regarding comparable situations. If you are working with a reputable search firm, your recruiter should be able to help you determine realistic expectations for your salary and benefits package. If you are not working with a recruiter but have one in your network, do not hesitate to contact that individual. Speaking personally, I am always happy to assist a former candidate or friend-of-a-friend who is considering a change of employer.

- **THE INTERNET.** Creative use of the internet can provide some information regarding comparable salaries although you have to be careful to use reputable sources. *Salary.com* and *jobsearch.about.com* are two sites that come to mind. In some cases, these sites will test your patience with various surveys and up-selling offers. But your research efforts can provide current information relating to compensation alternatives.

Perhaps the most important aspect of comparing two compensation packages is your own personal assessment of what is important. At different stages of your career, various components may increase or decrease in significance. To a non-golfer, a country club membership might be a glamorous but useless benefit. To an individual who is advanced in his or her career, retirement and/or severance benefits might be of great consequence. Someone supporting a family and a large mortgage might be less interested in long term/deferred compensation than in immediate cash flow. Appetite for outcome-based compensation might correlate to growing confidence in one's abilities.

Negotiating various components of a complex compensation package is a matter of give-and-take from both parties. Some companies will engage in significant trade-offs. Others will be more firm. If you are armed with research regarding comparable positions and some suggestions as to where you would like to end up, your chances of negotiating a better package increase.

---NEGOTIATING A BENEFITS PACKAGE---

- **VACATION.** Most companies offer a specific number of days for paid personal time based on years of work. It is my experience that there is little flexibility in this area, unless you are at the extreme upper levels of your company. No company wants to create discontent among its current employees by granting a newcomer additional vacation time. On the other hand, if you are leaving a position that offers 15 days of vacation and the new company has a standard of ten days, you should feel free to ask for matching time. Some companies will not officially budge, but may make informal arrangements to grant you several additional or unpaid days. Keep in mind that verbal commitments require a certain level of trust on your part that promises will be kept.

- **INSURANCE.** Similarly, health and other insurance benefits tend to be standard across a company. Some companies may or may not provide health or life insurance. Be sure to ask, as this is an important component of your compensation. If you are to be given a choice among various medical or life insurance plans, ask about what your choices will be and what each will cost. Be sure to evaluate your current and potential needs carefully.

- **RETIREMENT.** Retirement benefits at many companies consist of a 401k, matched by an employer up to a certain level of contribution. This can be a substantial amount and should be considered carefully when weighing competing job offers or comparing an offer to your current compensation. Generally, this benefit is not negotiable. A company is not required to provide any retirement benefits.

  Pensions, while very rare these days outside of government or unionized positions, might be a non-negotiable component of your compensation. Employees in their thirties and forties might not concern themselves with pensions and retirement benefits. But it is wise to remember that many employees who had no intention of remaining with a company for more than two or three years suddenly find themselves receiving gold watches at their retirement parties.

- **SEVERANCE.** A severance package is an agreement that a company will pay you a pre-determined amount if your employment is terminated by the company. A severance package may be a fixed amount or a length of time in which you will continue to receive a paycheck after your termination. A company is not required to provide a severance package. And most candidates will not concern themselves with a severance package at the point of accepting a job. (Fire ME??)

  If you are a low level employee, you can expect to get little or no severance pay. In most cases, if you are terminated for a specific cause, you will receive no more benefits than a cardboard box in which to stuff your personal belongings as you are escorted from the building. As your years of experience, your living expenses, and your salary increase, you should inquire about severance when negotiating a new offer.

---HOW MUCH IS TOO MUCH---

Negotiation is part and parcel of an executive job offer. It is expected and customary. Still, it can be a very sensitive process that will require all of your people skills. It is a talent to know just how far to go and when to stop asking for more.

Over the years, I have told candidates that negotiating a job offer is like placing your palm upon a pane of glass and pushing. The game is to push as hard as you can without breaking the glass. Once you break the figurative pane of glass, anything can happen and often does. The worst case is that the company rethinks its decision and rescinds your offer. At best, you may have started your tenure on bad note.

A friend of mine related a story about an executive who was recruited to a healthcare company located on the west coast. The candidate was a very good fit and had been well received by the CEO, COO and the Board. The wheels were put in motion and an offer was extended.

Feeling that he had a strong negotiating hand, the candidate requested several changes to the initial proposal. These additional requests were somewhat beyond what the members of the Board had originally intended to make available, but they acquiesced. A deal was struck and agreed to by all parties on a Friday. The following Monday, the candidate called to say that he had thought of one additional item over the weekend. He proposed that the company pay for his health club membership at a nearby private facility.

Hear the pane of glass breaking. When the Board members were made aware of the health club request, they rescinded the offer and started the search anew.

In the previous example, it was not the health club membership in and of itself that resulted in the rescission of the candidate's offer. It was "just one more" request after the Board had already granted numerous additional benefits.

So how much is too much in terms of negotiating? I am a golfer. Let me speak in terms of golf. Occasionally, as I am standing over a tough putt, a fellow golfer will advise me *"You have to hit it firmly!"* REALLY? How hard is firm? How firm is firm enough? How do I know just how much pressure to exert? The answer is, I am never sure until I have made or missed my putt. By then it is too late.

In regards to the negotiating process, I can only advise you to keep your eyes and ears open for clues that your negotiating pressure is reaching the breaking point. If you pile on a list of perks late in the negotiations, you had better prepare yourself for the tinkling sound of shattered glass.

---DECLINING AN OFFER---

As I have stated previously, it is best to remove yourself from a series of interviews as soon as you have enough information to determine that a position is not right for you. If that discovery has occurred during the first irritating words of the initial phone interview, you have the good fortune of walking away early in the process before anyone has wasted any time and effort. If your moment of truth comes later in the process when your future boss begins to whine and moan about your future staff, so be it. If it takes a miserly offer of employment to make you realize that your future place of employment is a sweat shop in a skyscraper, better now than later. As I stated earlier in this chapter, you should never begin negotiating an offer you do not intend to take.

But let's assume you have started negotiating in good faith for a job you have every intention of accepting. Unfortunately, you and the company fail to reach an accord on a key point of the offer and neither side is going to budge. You are left wondering what to do.

If you are suffering from an acute case of indecision, I suggest a time-out. Give yourself a few days to mull over the offer and arrive at a course of action.

> *If three or four days of torturing yourself do not make you comfortable with an offer, it is likely that nothing will. When your inner gyroscope is telling you something is wrong, it is wise to take heed.*

Once you have decided to decline an offer, the professional action, as uncomfortable as it may be, is to call the appropriate person at the company and inform that person of your decision. Do not decline an offer through e-mail. The hiring company has spent enough time with you to deserve a personal conversation regarding your decision.

The company representative may ask you if there is a specific problem relating to the offer. If such is the case, by all means speak up. But keep in mind that speaking up now is a commitment of sorts. If you bring up a problem which the company then resolves, the company will presume your acceptance of the offer. If you simply do not want the job and know it, do everyone a favor and decline without condition. While you may not receive a fond farewell as you hang up the phone, your own sense of relief will confirm that you have made the right choice and can begin to move along with your life and career.

---ACCEPTING AN OFFER---

If, on the other hand, you have received your job offer, evaluated every component carefully, negotiated several changes, and decided to accept a position, what happens next?

First, formalize the results of your negotiations. If you have made changes to the conditions in the original offer letter, ask for an updated letter, complete with the new, updated information. Your revised offer letter will probably express the company's happiness at your decision, and request you to confirm your formal acceptance of the offer by signing a copy of the letter and returning it via fax, mail or e-mail. The company may place a time limit of up to a week for your response. This date is firm. If you do not return the signed copy within the allotted deadline, the offer is officially rescinded.

Before you send off your signed letter of acceptance, you and the company should discuss and agree upon your start date. Hiring companies will generally expect an employed person to be available about two to three weeks from the offer acceptance date, allowing for fair notice at the candidate's current place of employment. If a candidate wishes to take some vacation time or other additional time before starting, this should be addressed now. An unemployed candidate should expect to start at the company's convenience. Excessive postponement of a start date by an employed or unemployed candidate may raise some eyebrows at the hiring company. *"A two-month wildlife safari???"*

---RESIGNING---

And now, the matter of resignation.

If you are leaving a job to take this role, you must tell your current employer as soon as possible. Let me share some quick thoughts on resignation.

Your employer will naturally prefer that you take your leave at your employer's convenience. The announcement of your departure may not come at a convenient time for your employer. In fact, if you are a responsible person in a responsible position, there may never be a convenient time for you to leave. So when you enter your boss's office to have that resignation conversation, be ready for a lively exchange.

A few companies routinely walk an individual off the premises on the day that notice of resignation is given. You should know if your company operates this way before you go in to resign. If so, have your personal effects either at home or in a box ready to go. If you have stored personal information on your company computer, make sure it has been removed.

Other companies celebrate an employee's success when that employee finds a better opportunity elsewhere. If your company abides by this policy, consider yourself fortunate. However, you may find yourself somewhat deflated when there is no visible sense of loss at the announcement of your departure. (Was that a sigh of relief you heard?) Such a company will wish you well and cooperate with you to arrange for an orderly transfer of duties.

In many cases, though, the departure of a key employee will gravely affect a department or a company. As you grow in importance to your company, you should anticipate some pushback in such a situation. Your resignation might elicit a response such as *"How can you do this to me/us?"* or *"I appreciate your situation but I would like to see if there is anything we can do to change your mind."*

In some cases, a company might extend a monetary counter-offer. It is wise to be prepared for this scenario in order to ensure that you achieve your desired outcome.

When you receive a counter-offer, it is critical to examine why you entertained the idea of leaving your current situation in the first place. Were you dissatisfied with the content of the job? That content will be as boring or tedious or stressful as ever. Were you leaving because there was no chance of upward mobility? Guess what – still no chance. Was your boss a raving lunatic? He or she will still be screaming at you daily. If salary was your one and only problem, a counter-offer might be able to "fix" that situation. But then why did you have to resign to get more money if the money was so readily available? Be careful. It is awfully difficult to think clearly when everyone is telling you that you are the prettiest girl at the prom.

If your employer, faced with your imminent departure, accelerates existing plans to boost your career, you should be receptive. A promotion will enhance both your resume and your breadth of experience. At this point, you must evaluate your new title with your current employer versus your competing job offer. It is imperative that you make a speedy decision. Do not play games for fear of alienating both your current and potential employer.

---SUMMARY---

Receiving a job offer is an exciting event, and one that occurs only rarely in most people's careers. You should feel pleased and flattered, but you should avoid letting your emotions prevail over practical considerations. Here are a few general guidelines relating to negotiating job offers:

- Know all of your current compensation components and their value.
- Do not begin to negotiate an offer for a job that is not a good fit.
- Early in your career, there are fewer negotiating options.
- Be prepared to justify any requests for higher salary.

- Research compensation data relating to comparable positions.
- Use your people skills to know when to stop asking for embellishments to an offer.
- Get an offer in writing before resigning your current position.
- When resigning from your current position, be prepared for every scenario.

INTERVIEW MASTER

Interviewer:

Chad, you drive a hard bargain. Your deal is well above what I and the Board anticipated extending. But I have to say, you presented a great case for every item and won us over. We look forward to having you on the team.

Candidate:

Thank you. The good news is that from now on, I will have <u>our</u> best interests in mind as I negotiate on behalf of the Company.

Chapter 16

70 Interview Quick Tips:
If you only read one chapter,
make it this one

INTERVIEW DISASTER

Recruiter:

We would like to schedule an initial interview for tomorrow or Friday. Would you be able to work with that schedule?

Candidate:

Sure, no problem. Tomorrow at 10 a.m. works. I look forward to seeing you. Now what was the name of your company again?

Throughout this book, I have attempted to preach the ways and means, the whys and whos and hows of succeeding at a job interview. This chapter is for those who prefer very short sermons. (You "cut-to-the-chase" types – you know who you are.)

---PREPARING FOR ENTRY---

1. In the days preceding the interview, use the internet to find out all you can about the company in which you will be interviewing.

2. Prior to the day of the interview, map out the directions to the interview location. Plan your drive/commute time accordingly. Getting lost or calling for directions in the hour preceding the interview is not a way to impress the interviewer with your planning and time management skills.

3. Read the newspaper on the day of your interview. At some point during your interview process, it will be helpful to be able to make small talk about the day's events.

4. If available, memorize the name(s) of your interviewer(s).

5. Arrive at the appointed location between five and fifteen minutes before the interview begins. Do not arrive a half hour early; do not arrive one minute late. If you find yourself in the parking lot well before the interview begins, drive around the area or find a place where you can sit unobserved and have a cup of coffee. If necessary, find a restroom before entering the interview location.

6. You may not be as attractive as a model, but you should look like you have just finished a photo shoot when you arrive. Your hair should be clean and combed; your clothing should be freshly cleaned and pressed; your shoes should be shiny; there should be no evidence of perspiration. If it is a rainy day, be sure you have protected your perfect look with an umbrella or a raincoat.

7. Bring a briefcase or portfolio containing extra copies of your resume in case they are needed. You should also bring a pen and a pad of paper.

---ARRIVAL---

8. As soon as you walk into the outer office or reception area, be aware that everything you do or say is being scrutinized. You are the goldfish in the fish bowl; the gymnast on the balance beam; the golfer over a putt. From this point forward, your words and demeanor should emanate professionalism and dignity.

9. When you enter the reception area, address the receptionist with friendliness and respect. Introduce yourself in a clear, confident voice.

"Hi. I am John Adams and I have a 9:00 appointment with Tom Jefferson," is as clear as you can get. There is no need to state that you are here for a job interview unless the receptionist volunteers the information first. The receptionist will probably direct you to have a seat while you wait for Mr. Jefferson.

10. Ask the receptionist where to hang any outerwear so that when summoned, you can proceed directly into your interview.

11. Choose a chair that will allow you to sit straight and stand gracefully when called for your interview. Do not sprawl out across a low couch. Standing is acceptable.

12. If you make conversation with the receptionist, make sure it is as light and fluffy as angel food cake. Refrain from anything but innocuous small talk. The receptionist is not a bartender and is probably not interested in your life story or personal problems. Remember: anything you say can and will be used against you when receptionist reports to the boss; odd or obnoxious comments will not go unnoticed.

13. Be still. You are a professional. Do not pace the room or repeatedly leave the office as you wait for your appointment. Turn off your cell phone. Do not read the novel you always carry in your briefcase, although you are free to browse through magazines in the reception area. If you haven't done so (shame on you), this might be a good time to review your resume and prepare for questions.

14. If 20 minutes pass and you have not been called into the interview or advised of a delay, it is fair to ask the receptionist for a status update. Keep in mind that time passes slowly while you are in waiting mode. Make sure 20 minutes have passed.

15. The moment you are summoned, you are bound to experience a rapid heartbeat or two. Recognize that this is normal. Less normal would be to not experience a small attack of nervousness. Remind yourself that the person you will be speaking to is just another human being who may be just as uncomfortable with the interviewing process as you are. It may also be helpful to remember that your background has already been evaluated and deemed acceptable for the specified position.

16. With as little commotion as possible, rise and walk confidently to meet your interviewer.

---GREETING---

17. Immediately make eye contact with your interviewer. It is extremely difficult to establish a rapport with someone who is constantly looking off to the side or downward. If you are aware that you have this habit, work beforehand on looking people directly in the eye when you are speaking.

18. Extend your hand for a handshake. Your handshake should be firm, but not bone-crushing. Your hands and nails should be clean. If your hands tend to perspire, keep a tissue in your pocket and subtly squeeze it before you greet your interviewer. A limp handshake will rightly or wrongly be seen as a negative. A meek handshake is generally not seen as a plus when you are interviewing for a professional job.

19. Your interviewer will state his name. *Good morning, I'm Tom Jefferson."*

20. At this point, you will need to determine whether to address your interviewer by first or last name. I suggest that, if you are very young (20s) and/or there is more that a 15-year age difference, you begin using the more formal Mr. or Ms. salutation, and wait for permission to address your interviewer on a first-name basis.

21. Return your interviewer's greeting, stating your name clearly.

22. Smile when you introduce yourself. You are trying to appear cool, confident and professional, but not unfriendly.

23. As you approach the interview setting, be prepared to make a few minutes of small talk regarding the weather, the traffic, or a sporting event. Avoid the subject of how horrific the commute was from your home to the interview location. Avoid babbling. Small talk should be a 50-50 give-and-take exchange.

24. Your interviewer will direct you to be seated. Sit straight in your chair. Your demeanor should be attentive, wide-awake, ready!

25. Quickly scan the office for personal items of the interviewer (pictures, plaques, certificates) that may give you insight into that person's interests or mutual experiences. These can be conversation starters.

---IN A MANNER OF SPEAKING---

26. For the duration of the interview, keep in mind that this is a business meeting, not a conversation between friends. Do not get too comfortable and let your guard down.
27. Having said that, do not appear cold and unfriendly. Try to establish a professional rapport.
28. Maintain an even, calm tone while speaking. Your volume should be moderate and measured.
29. Do not gesticulate wildly while speaking.
30. Maintain reasonable eye contact with your interviewer while you are speaking and while he/she is speaking to you.
31. Do not mumble.
32. To the best of your ability, try to use correct grammar.
33. Avoid slang, profanity, and non-existent words. If you are not sure how to pronounce a word, do not use it.
34. Try not to punctuate your sentences with superfluous words such as *"like"* and *"you know."*
35. Do not be a comedian. A few humorous remarks are acceptable and even attractive during the interview, but should not dominate your presentation. Certainly any jokes that might be considered by anyone in the world to be tasteless or offensive or stupid should be avoided. Self-deprecating jokes are not recommended in an interview setting.
36. Take a few notes if necessary, but your focus should be on the back-and-forth exchange of ideas. You might need to jot down a name, phone number, a web address, or other piece of contact information.

37. Provide enough personal/family information to assure your interviewer that you are not in the witness protection program, but refrain from providing too many details. Your interviewer does not need to know if you and your wife are having problems or if you are dealing with a family member who is seriously ill or what church you attend.

---ANSWERING QUESTIONS---

38. Place a copy of your resume in your lap or in a portfolio for easy reference regarding chronology, dates, and details.
39. Listen carefully and concentrate on what is asked. An interview is not the time to let your mind wander.
40. Answer questions as directly as you can. Do not evade or avoid specific questions.
41. Answer all questions truthfully. A lie can destroy your career.
42. If you are not sure what your interviewer is looking for, it is acceptable to ask for clarification.
43. Try to confine your answers to roughly two minutes.
44. Stay on point. Some people exhibit nervousness by rambling. If you find yourself providing irrelevant or unnecessary information, rein yourself in.
45. One-word or very-short answers will not suffice either. Yes and No will not convince an employer to hire you over your competition.
46. Provide real-life examples to support your statements. For instance, if you state, *"I regard myself as an excellent manager of people,"* you should provide details of a people management situation that you handled well.
47. Incorporate meaningful statistics in your answers whenever possible. If you sold 150% of your sales quota each year, mention it. If you decreased production time per unit by 30%, tell about it. Numbers provide unbiased support for your accomplishments.
48. Emphasize your achievements. You do not need to rehash every menial duty you ever performed.
49. Fly over your distant past; focus on your most recent positions.

50. Focus specifically on responsibilities you have had that are relevant to this opportunity.

51. If you are asked a question to which you don't have an immediate answer, give yourself a few seconds to think. Not every answer will be your best answer. That's okay. Sometimes, you will be judged as much on your poise as on the content of your answer.

52. Be prepared to answer tough questions, particularly about the less positive aspects of your resume. For instance, if you have changed jobs often; accepted a demotion; were laid off; were unemployed for a long period; all of these will be questioned. (See Chapter 11.) Do not become flustered. Answer truthfully and try to phrase your answers in a manner that will reflect positively on you. Remember that the company has already seen all the blemishes on your resume and still decided to invite you to interview.

---ASKING QUESTIONS---

53. Be prepared to ask some specific questions that demonstrate your knowledge of and interest in the company. Some examples of this are: *"How many people work at your plant in Mexico?"* or *"Do you have any new products being released into the market this year"* or *"Is your management strategy more centralized or de-centralized?"*

54. Ask questions about your role, especially questions that will help you determine your interest in the position. Some examples:
"To what extent does this role have attention of upper management?"
"How many staff members does this position manage?"
"Where is the person who had this role most recently?"
"What future avenues might be available within the company for someone who excels in this role?"
"What percent of the job requires travel?"
"What would the yardstick be when gauging success in this position a year from now?"

55. Ask questions that demonstrate your expertise in the competencies required by the position.

56. Ask something. A lack of curiosity or interest in the position will almost always be construed as a negative.
57. There IS such a thing as a stupid question. That would be one pertaining to an issue the interviewer has already addressed.

---DISCUSSING SALARY AND BENEFITS---

58. If you have not already covered the subject in your initial phone contact, you will need to ask what the salary range is for this position. Your interviewer will probably provide this information. You may indicate your level of satisfaction at the range or, if the range is disappointing, ask if there is any upward extension possible. Hint: Get an idea of salary range before you commit to an interview.
59. Conversely, if the interviewer asks you about your salary requirements, you may answer with an acceptable range. Or you might counter with a question regarding the salary range being offered, and then respond to that information. *"I would be satisfied with the upper level of your range"* or *"I had hoped to make a little more than that"* are both appropriate responses.
60. If the interviewer asks directly about your most recent salary, you must provide the truthful answer. Failure to provide the answer is likely to eliminate you from consideration.
61. It is reasonable to ask about the working environment, including the length of the work day. Ask a question such as *"What are the stated office hours?"* or *"How would you describe a typical work day?"* Your interviewer will probably use this as an opportunity to tell you about overtime expectations.
62. If you are interviewing for a high ranking executive position, your interest in the official working hours should be minimal, as you can expect to work as many hours as are required to fulfill your responsibilities.

63. Should the role call for "excessive" overtime, it is reasonable to ask if this is a short term solution to business demands or part of the operating strategy. It will be your decision as to whether this is acceptable but you will know the game at the outset.

64. Do not ask about vacation, insurance or other benefits at the first interview. Defer these questions until a later interview or receipt of an offer.

---END GAME---

65. As the meeting winds down, be prepared to summarize in about one to two minutes why your background and credentials make you a terrific fit for the employer's position.

66. When asked if you are interested in pursuing the position, almost always answer affirmatively. There is no use wasting the time you just spent unless you are absolutely, positively, undeniably sure you will never set foot in the company's doorway again. You can, of course, change your mind when you get home and notify the company via e-mail of your change of heart.

67. A big smile, a firm handshake, eye contact, and a sincere thank you for the time the interviewer has made available to you will close out your interview in a positive fashion.

---AFTERWARD---

68. Send thank-you notes or e-mails to each person you met.

69. If a recruiter is involved, contact that person to debrief the details of your meeting(s).

70. Get comfortable and wait patiently for feedback.

INTERVIEW MASTER

Interviewer:

You have made a great impression on everybody you met with today. You were very well prepared and appeared very relaxed.

Candidate:

I felt very comfortable in every meeting. It was as though I knew exactly what would happen and what would be asked.

Acknowledgements

Over my years in the executive search business, many people suggested that I write a book. I want to thank those people for planting the seed that resulted in this book.

Jim Fitzgerald, who penned the prologue for this book, has been a business associate, coach and friend for many years. His monthly inquiry, "How's the book coming?" was the sometimes annoying nudge I needed to plow through what had to be done. I cannot thank Jim enough for his honest comments, support and interest.

Several individuals were called upon for the unglamorous job of reading the various iterations of the developing manuscript. Their input helped to make the final product much more enjoyable and is appreciated beyond words. Cynthia and I want to extend a heartfelt thank you to Greg Szatko, Ramona Robert, Barbara Ward, Kaylee Putbrese, Beth Scheidler, Kaelan Ward, Don Pearson, and Jim Shanahan for their time and thoughts.

Finally, we would like to thank all of the individuals including Steve Garrett, Paul Zellner, Michael McCurdy, Michael Grabowski, and Dr. John Gaski PhD, who were so generous with their time. Many people were very gracious in sharing their opinions and experiences, which found their way into this book.

Bob Ward
January, 2011

Footnotes

Footnote 1

I first heard this quote in a speech given by Mr. Zig Ziglar in Rosemont, Illinois. I later learned that the phrase was based upon the title of a book written by his younger brother, Judge Ziglar: *Timid salesmen have skinny kids* (Action Now, Inc. 1978).

Footnote 2

Magnum Force, 1973, director Ted Post, released by Warner Brothers. Quote delivered by Clint Eastwood as the character, Dirty Harry.

About the Authors

Bob Ward has been an executive recruiter for over 25 years. His firm, Ward & Associates, provides dedicated search services to clients in a variety of industries. He has personally observed and participated in hundreds of job interviews, providing guidance and direction to both hiring managers and candidates.

A Chicago native and graduate of The University of Notre Dame, Mr. Ward began his career as a CPA with PriceWaterhouseCoopers. He subsequently held financial management positions with several real estate and retail companies and worked with a national recruitment firm before founding Ward & Associates in 1994.

Cynthia Ward is a graduate of the University of Illinois with a degree in Communications/Advertising. She joined Ward & Associates as a researcher on a full-time basis in 2005.

Ward & Associates executes searches for individuals with unique experience for closely-held and publicly traded companies throughout the United States.

Ward & Associates
www.robertward.com
Naperville, Illinois

7377231R0

Made in the USA
Charleston, SC
24 February 2011